OVERCOMING *Mediocrity*

5 out of 5 Stars

It's a Great Investment in Yourself

"This is an inspiring compilation. Each woman's story contains powerful lessons that are widely applicable. Heartwarming and triumphant all at the same time. Any woman who's tread a rocky path on her life's journey will be able to relate and rejoice along with each author as she overcomes adversity and challenge. If you're seeking inspiration to overcome adversity, take a moment to breathe, regroup, and soak up a story or three. It's a great investment in yourself."

—Debbra

5 out of 5 Stars

Highly Recommend!!

"HIGHLY RECOMMEND!!! If you are looking for personal and professional development, this book is for you! It is perfectly inspiring, educational, empowering and beautifully written! I could really relate to the struggles in their personal stories and it has helped me to continue working on overcoming my own obstacles so I can succeed in life and in business! Thank you all for sharing your incredible journeys."

—Lisa

5 out of 5 Stars

Inspired, Raw Stories from the Heart

"Inspiring! As someone who cares about helping people in a purposeful way, I continually find myself reminded that everyone has a story. What is unique about "Resilient Women Overcoming Mediocrity" is that each woman's (life) chapter differs in remarkable ways—their family dynamics, circumstances, and work experiences—and yet chose the option of going into business for themselves (often despite immense odds) and came out remarkably well on the other side.

Through raw sharing, they willingly own their history-no easy feat! I highly recommend this book for any woman who is looking for support, another way, or camaraderie and who may struggle in her own path; someone who finds inspiration from others who have overcome often great challenges and have paved the way for the rest of us. There is a difference between mediocrity and adversity. These authors have set the bar to overcome both. Kudos to all."

—Brenda

4 out of 5 Stars

A Book of Empowering and Inspiring Stories by Women!

"This book is full of amazing stories of women who have overcome adversity in different ways. They have gone above and beyond the usual and succeeded in discovering their talents and power to do whatever they put their minds to. These incredible women display a strength of character and stamina and perseverance needed in a tough competitive world. I found this book to be inspiring and quite enjoyable. The women each have different personalities but there is one thread that is the same - their determination to succeed in their chosen fields.

I would recommend this book to all women whether they are in business or not to help them believe in themselves—believe that even the impossible is possible!"

—Jjspina

5 out of 5 Stars
This Book Is Great! It Really Motivated Me.

"This book is great! It really motivated me to take the next step with my life and career. All of these women have accomplished so much, and I strive to be like them. We can all achieve greatness if we put in a little effort!"

—Amazon Customer

5 out of 5 Stars
Excellent Read for Men and Women!

"LOVED THE BOOK! [Husband] thought it should not be limited to a "women's" book—excellent for men and women. Writing was personal, intimate, yet clearly educational in nature. Long enough to take you somewhere, but short enough to sit down and read right then. The book is downloaded on our Kindle so we can read again."

—TJ

5 out of 5 Stars
Hope and Faith

"I loved this very inspirational book. All of the women had such different stories. I ordered another copy for a Christmas gift. It's exactly what we all need to remind us that we can overcome with faith."

—Amazon Customer

What our clients are saying about...

OVERCOMING
Mediocrity.

"I'm passionate about helping women overcome the lies that are holding them back. The problem was that I still believed my own lies. I questioned if my story could actually make a difference, feared that no one would want to hear it and didn't trust I could write it well enough for it to be published. Until I met Christie. She invited me to share my story in one of her books, and it completely transformed my business, my life and best of all, the lives of the women who read it. They've reached out to me, grateful for how what I shared helped them overcome their adversities. Hearing those women's testimonies gave me confidence and fueled me to keep writing. With Christie's help, I published my own book just a few months later, and am currently writing the next in that series."

—Shannon Ferraby
Author, Speaker & Trainer with Success Unwrapped
Overcoming Mediocrity Influential Women

"Working with Christie and her team was just the nudge I needed to finally sit down and start writing. The social media tips that were provided when the book launched were also invaluable for engaging and re-engaging people who follow me. I am much more confident about my next book, and it's launch."

—Valerie Mrak
Speaker • Filmmaker • Storyteller • Coach
Overcoming Mediocrity Victorious Women

"I am an Amazon Best Selling Author! How cool is that? Just to let you know, there are more people than my mother and myself that care about that. It makes a difference to my clients!

Being an author in the series has opened doors for me. It makes it easier to rise to the top of the list for those responsible for booking speaking gigs to want to talk to me. The traffic to my website and Business Page has increased measurably. It has shortened the know, like, trust factor. People are reaching out to me first, before I reach out to them. The titles of the books help women who want to stretch themselves. Who wouldn't want to associate themselves and work with an author who is Dynamic, Resilient, Strong and Influential?"

—Jeanne Lyons
Career Breakthrough Coach
Overcoming Mediocrity Influential Women

"My motto is, if you are not having fun, you are doing something wrong. Christie and the DPWN Team made the publishing process so seamless and, dare I say fun because they have created a system that is working. All I had to do was to follow the bouncing smiley face (not literally of course).

When I learned about this project, I was already fully into the writing, publishing and marketing process of my other book, Getting Yourself Unstuck. However, I couldn't put everything in that book. Therefore, Overcoming Mediocrity *allowed me to publish a very personal story that didn't seem to fit in my other book. Now going forward in my marketing, the two books will work in tandem."*

—Angie Engstrom
Coach and Plank Trainer
Overcoming Mediocrity Resilient Women

"Christie and the OM team took an overwhelming and complicated process of book publishing and made it very easy to get my story published. I was guided through the process from start to finish. Every detail was outlined, and my questions were always answered promptly. The book has received rave reviews, and it has taken my credibility to the next level, as I am now an Amazon #1 best seller! Thank you!!"

—Lynn O'Dowd
Motivational Speaker and Keynote Performer
Overcoming Mediocrity Influential Women

OVERCOMING MEDIOCRITY

FEARLESS WOMEN

OVERCOMING *Mediocrity*©

**A unique collection of stories from fearless women
who have created their own lives of significance!**

Presented by Christie L. Ruffino

DPWN Publishing

www.OvercomingMediocrity.org

This book is a compilation of stories from numerous experts who have each contributed a chapter. It is designed to provide information and inspiration to our readers.

It is sold with the understanding that the publisher and the individual authors are not engaged in the rendering of psychological, legal, accounting or other professional advice. The content and views in each chapter are the sole expression and opinion of its author and not necessarily the views of DPWN Publishing, Christie Lee Ruffino or the Dynamic Professional Women's Network, Inc.

For more information, contact:
DPWN Publishing
A division of the Dynamic Professional Women's Network, Inc.
1879 N. Neltnor Blvd. #316, West Chicago, IL 60185
www.OvercomingMediocrity.org
www.OurDPWN.com

Printed in the United States of America

ISBN: 978-1-939794-28-4

Dedication

To every woman who does not believe she can make a difference; and to every woman who believes she can move a mountain.

To every woman who continually makes sacrifices for those she loves; and to every woman who prioritizes those moments, when she can pamper and take care of her own needs.

To every woman who believes that she should settle for the life she has; and to every woman who has overcome great odds to create her own life of significance.

To the fearless women in this book who've shared their stories with you; in hopes that their lessons of pain will become your lessons of power.

To the women in my life who believe I am significant and who I believe are priceless.

The Power of a Story

There is nothing more important in this world than the relationships we build and the legacy we leave in the lives of those who've crossed paths with us on our journey of life. It's the experiences we have during this journey that define our individual uniqueness and create our own powerful personal blueprint or our unique story snowflake.

It is this blueprint that can empower and equip us to possess a distinct advantage over every other person in this world, if leveraged correctly and shared. If we don't have the courage to share our snowflake, it will be lost forever. No one will have the same story, and no one can repeat your story. Therefore, those who come after you, will never learn anything from what you've experienced and what you've learned.

I feel that the most significant thing we can do to add value back to this world, is to master the narrative of our lives. All of our leadership and moneymaking abilities rest in our ability to discover, craft and deliver our personal story or message in a way that will allow people to connect to us. The right story shared at the right time with the right person can alter the trajectory of their life, as well as our own.

We can also learn from other people's stories to change the direction of our own story and to redirect our ultimate destiny.

Power to you and the story of your life!

"Everything you want is on the other side of fear."

—Jack Canfield

Introduction

When I embarked upon this journey, never in my wildest dreams did I expect it to turn out as it has. My motives were grand, yet much more simplistic than they are today.

My initial goal was to create one co-authored book, collecting stories from women I admired who were members of my organization, the Dynamic Professional Women's Network (DPWN). I knew how sharing my story in a similar book (compiled by a mentor of mine, Michelle Prince) had been transformational for me. I also knew how having a book to share in the business community gave me additional credibility, recognition, and exposure. What I didn't know was how these same stories would be just as transformational for the readers, as they related with one or more of the women who were willing to share their stories in such a vulnerable and authentic way.

I also had no way of knowing how working with these women would lead me down a path that would change 'my' life forever…

My Story

I'm a natural connector. Many women are. I believe it is a part of our DNA to connect people with other people or resources that can help them. Many times, I've shared how my journey to build DPWN was not intentional. As an introvert, the last thing I wanted to do was build a business, where I would have to frequently talk with new people… strangers. However, thankfully, God knew better than I did what was best for me.

Now, 16 years later, our community is thriving in the Chicagoland area. We have also expanded into other states. We have a fierce online presence with virtual meetings, on-demand training and Mastermind Success Circles. You can connect with us at www.OurDPWN.com.

Personally, I work with women who are on a quest to build a profitable and impactful business as a coach, author and speaker. That's my passion and where my story has brought me thus far. I'm blessed to wake up every day, knowing that I can help my clients live into THEIR passion; which is to help their clients. We're creating a wonderful ripple effect. You can connect with me at www.ChristieRuffino.com.

Our *Overcoming Mediocrity* series of books is going just as strong, celebrating book number eight, featuring an amazing lineup of fearless women. The stories in each of our books are about strength, faith and courage. They are about having the confidence to believe in ourselves, even when those we love may not. They're about having the courage to do hard things, even when we don't want to. They're also about remaining fearless through all of life's ups and downs, because that is what, as women, we do brilliantly. Do you have a story of strength, faith or courage? You can connect with us at www. OvercomingMediocrity.org.

Your Story

What is your story? ARE YOU LIVING YOUR STORY? Or are you living for someone else's story? Maybe you ARE living into your destiny. Or maybe you spend the majority of your time unhappily working for someone else, taking care of someone else, or doing something that does not create a fire in your soul. You're managing, thinking… one of these days, it will be my turn. What if that time never comes?

The personal and professional development industry generates billions of dollars of revenue every year. According to www.marketresearch.com, the U.S. estimated market value for personal coaching was $955 million in 2015 and $1.02 billion in 2016. This market value is expected to reach $1.34 billion by 2022, which represents a 6.7% average yearly growth rate.

The great news is that for every one of those coaches, there are countless people desperately searching for help.

I work with women who have reached a point in their lives, where they're finally ready to step into their destiny, own their story and share their wisdom. They are women who don't think they have the skills to become a coach, but they know down deep in their gut that they can help people. They're considering stepping into a coaching or consulting role, but they don't know where to start, or they've been trying, and they're just not getting the results they desire (or frankly that they deserve).

If you just read that and felt a butterfly or two swirling around in your stomach, then maybe we should chat. I have a simple system that will provide you with the steps and support to build a profitable business as a coach, author and speaker.

Our Books—Their Story

Our first *Overcoming Mediocrity* book was a smashing success! On the very first day of its release in 2013, it became the #1 downloaded Kindle book in the motivational genre category. Twenty-two women shared their stories to inspire other women to overcome and succeed as they had, and all authors were able to claim the distinguished Amazon Bestselling Author status.

Because of the overwhelming success of that first book, we went on to produce additional books under the *Overcoming Mediocrity* brand. Each of them also climbed to the #1 position on Amazon on the very first day of release. Two of them, *Overcoming Mediocrity—Resilient Women* and *Influential Women*, both reached the #1 position in two categories, which was a great accomplishment.

These books have ultimately taken on a life of their own and have made a greater impact than ever anticipated. It is exciting to read testimonials from women who have read and connected with one or more of the inspirational stories inside. It's even more exciting when one of those same women decide to share their story in one of our future books.

It is now with great honor and pride, that I can share stories from the fearless women in this book. I have had the pleasure of getting to know each of these ladies and learning a little about the stories they're sharing with you. I'm deeply inspired by the courage they're exhibiting. They are sharing the personal details of their lives, with the sole intention of allowing you, the reader, to learn from their experiences and wisdom.

It is easy to become complacent. Live a life of mediocrity, just coasting through day by day. It takes courage to fight through the hard and overcome challenges that seem impossible to defeat. The women in the pages of this book made a purposeful choice to live significant lives and share their stories, to help you also live a life of significance. This demonstrates strength, humility and the heart of a true go-giver. These women all have even greater things yet to come. They are women whom you should know, learn from and emulate.

This book is meant to not only encourage you but to also awaken your inner desire to share your story along with them. Each woman in our project wants to make the biggest possible impact in the world and transform as many lives as possible, by sharing their story and wisdom in a book that will get massive exposure. They could have kept their stories private; that would have been the safest and easiest path for them. However, they decided to step out of their comfort zone and share the narratives of their lives with you. We invite you to join them on this journey.

I am blessed to have the opportunity to share these fearless women with you. I hope you feel just as blessed to receive the value they offer you.

Hugs & Blessings,

Christie

Table of Contents

Donna Eller

Choosing Love as a Way of Life

I remember the moment it happened, the instant that I got that I have a choice of being right or acting out of love or, another way of saying it is, *Choosing Love as a Way of Life*.

Even though it was half a lifetime ago, the memory is extremely vivid. It feels as if it was yesterday for me.

I am posed on a slimy rock, the blue-green water lapping at my bare feet. Each splash threatens to loosen my toes' grip. I'm in Aruba, gazing back at the light pink, salty sand from my perch on the rock in the ocean. I see a line of mothers, each holding a baby or small child, every one of them hoping theirs will be chosen for the cover shot. The only danger they see is that their baby might start to cry and then they will not get the cover. The danger I see is the slimy rock, my slippery feet, and the possibility that I could lose my grip, and plunge, with their child, into the sea hurting them, me or both.

Raging in the back of my mind is, "I am 33-years old, and I need this cover."

I'd been a top fashion model for a decade, my chiseled cheeks and blonde hair praised in print, my photographs are seen in *Vogue*, *Harper's Bazaar*, and many other magazines. Now, aware that I was nearing the life-expectancy of a model, I was cautious and careful to do exactly what was asked of me. This cover shoot for *McCall's* Magazine, with a circulation of millions, was vital for my career.

I won the cover, and it catapulted me to the next stage in my career. I didn't feel good about it, and I still don't feel good about it. This inner conflict was a tipping point for me.

In my portfolio, there were shots of me modeling for Armani, Vidal Sassoon and Bloomingdale's. I felt that I was *right* to stay in the editorial world of modeling. I didn't want to be shoved into the world of older models and having to play mommy roles in catalogs. I had also violated my integrity, by not speaking up and standing for beautiful older models. That moment seared my soul.

Professionally, that *McCall's* cover tipped me into what is called the Sophisticated Division of modeling. My being in this division created jobs, like playing a pregnant mother, painting a child's room for Sears, or appearing in maternity catalogs. The jobs changed from editorial to sophisticated women bookings. For that, financially, I was grateful.

Personally, however, it was a Norma Rae moment. I sensed that it was time for me to stand in my own power, and to embolden younger models. They get put into questionable situations on the job, and they think—because they're between fifteen and twenty years old when they start—that they *have* to do that job. This is because there is no one behind them saying that they *do* have a choice and they *can* say No.

In that moment, standing on that slimy rock, with babies being passed, one by one, onto my hip, I went from someone who didn't have a voice, to someone who did. I can choose, I realized. I do have a choice, and I wanted models everywhere to have a choice about what is safe and what isn't.

The economic climate at that time was challenging, to say the least. My modeling agency, IMG, shut its doors. There was a stock market crash on Wall Street. And, I was at *that* age—you know *that* age, where you aren't sought after.

I shifted from a fear-laden litany of "I'm going to be a single, white, stupid North Carolina model, about to be homeless, and broke on the streets of New York" to "no, I don't get to do that. There is too much to be responsible for in this industry." I had to deal with my imperfect self, and I got really committed to the modeling industry. The thought that the modeling industry doesn't protect children, evolved into building the first workers' union for models.

I co-founded "The Models Guild, Local 51" in 1995, with a woman who wanted to be a model, Amie Bongay. One of the main reasons I joined forces with Amie, was that the fashion agencies didn't provide us with health insurance, dental insurance, pensions, life insurance or workers' compensation. Some of the fly-by-night agencies were known to force girls to spend thousands of dollars for their portfolios with promises of work, and then didn't get them any work. Teenage girls were steered into prostitution and forced into drugs. Modeling agencies were duping the girls. Even worse, Amie had gotten raped as a girl, while trying to become a model.

For the hundreds of models who didn't make the six-figures per day that Cindy Crawford, Christy Turlington, and Beverly Johnson did at that time, life for us was twelve-hour days, uncertainty over where to live in the Big Apple and abusing our bodies to stay skinny. When I resisted going to the sophisticated division, to stay competitive as a working model, at five-feet-nine inches, my weight plunged from 128 pounds to 103 pounds. I wanted to look like what I thought they wanted me to look like, to stay in the editorial division.

Amie and I didn't stop at unionizing. We crammed a bus full of models and drove to Albany, New York from Manhattan. We convinced the state legislature to pass laws protecting models of all ages. The lawmakers agreed, and, finally, child models were getting their much-needed breaks, tutoring and food.

We were also getting modeling agencies shut down, and we were forcing fly-by-night agencies who scammed girls out of their money, to pay up. Meanwhile, my modeling career took me to Wilhelmina, where I was moved off editorial. No longer in the fashion magazines, I was now in the sophisticated division, with the older models.

We started getting threats. So did the Models Guild, and the girls were getting scared. Many of them were afraid to be involved in the union. A growing number of models pushed ahead. I figured that my career was pretty much over anyway. Why not get us health insurance?

What I got—along with the health insurance—was news coverage. On *60-Minutes*, the focus was on models' fights with anorexia and bulimia. The Models Guild was on *The New York Minute* about forty-five times. I was on with the NBC *Today Show's* Matt Lauer. *Hard Copy* covered the story about The Models Guild putting the head of a fashion agency behind bars, for embezzling from the models and for statutory rape.

It was quite an adventure for a girl who grew up in a small farming town, with a population of 10,000 in North Carolina. I have two brothers. Tarboro was my mother's hometown. While Tarboro was my home base, we didn't stay there. My dad was in the Air Force, so I was lucky enough to also be an Air Force brat. I was actually born in England. We also lived in Japan, Florida and Utah. Every few years, we moved back to my mom's hometown.

That global influence helped me in both school and in the modeling world. All that coming and going, made me realize I wanted a skillset of making friends quickly. I figured I'd be moving soon, so I'd better get related fast. I call it instant relatedness. Consequently, I had friends around the world. Home is where I am.

Home, after high school graduation, was Florida, where I attended Bauder College. That only lasted a couple of years. It was long enough to get my associate degree. This is because, on a visit to New York City, I got scooped up by Click and Foster-Fell, my first modeling agency.

My education was interrupted, but my fashion modeling career was on fire. I was a Fit model at first, with designers trying their gowns on me. Then, I did runway, and, when my modeling agency sent me to Milan, suddenly, my career took off. I spent eight years in Europe, modeling in London, Milan,

Paris, Hamburg, Munich and Amsterdam.

My high-fashion years had me clad in Ann Taylor, Donna Karan, Armani, Eddie Bauer, Land's End, La Perla and Victoria's Secret. I modeled for Bloomingdale's and Macy's. My face and hair—in colors from blonde to red to raven—were treated by make-up artists and stylists from Clairol, Vidal Sassoon, Oil of Olay and Dove soap. My image danced on—and inside—the covers of *Vogue, Harper's Bazaar, Self, Woman's Day, Good Housekeeping* and *McCall's*. This is not to mention *Donna Magazine, Italian Vogue Sposa, Mode,* and *GQ*.

These were heady days for a girl in her twenties, one who felt incredibly insecure. As much as I lived all over the world, I was in my own world. I was self-absorbed and scared. My attention was on my insecurities, my career and partying.

But, it wasn't until posing for that *McCall's* cover—with that heightened sense of danger for the infants placed in my arms—that it couldn't be just about me anymore. In my head, I heard the words, "Get your f***ing attention off yourself! You could hurt this child."

That moment ripped off the blinders. I realized that I had to start taking care of my body. I comfortably moved from a size six to a size eight. I started loving who I was. This was ironic, since this was also the time when my world started crashing in on me—with IMG closing down, the stock market crash, and turning thirty-three years old.

At that moment, I saw that I could be a tipping point for the human spirit. *That* was my job in the world, not modeling for fashion magazines. It was a shift from having all my attention on myself, to having attention on others. That perspective evolved out of a challenging training program that wouldn't allow me to stay small and self-involved. My perspective became, "Who do I get to be for others?"

Whether the other models were younger or slimmer, older or heavier, there was no separation between any of us. One of my first acts out of that shift of consciousness, was that I would stand up for all of us. I could speak. I have a voice. When we are passionate about what we do, we don't sell out. If we have the ability to have a voice, we would always act out of love.

Instead of being under the control of someone telling me where to show up and what to do, I stepped into being a businesswoman. I literally started seeing opportunities to be a keynote speaker, to teach courses and to coach clients into building the lives they truly wanted. I started taking on my career in a different way.

I was no longer the fearful woman struggling to keep her grip on a slimy rock out at sea. I was able to balance moviemaking, modeling, suiting Wall Street men and unionizing.

While still modeling for Wilhelmina, I was also Co-founder and Executive Producer of The Models Guild, Local 51, OPEIU (the Office and Professional Employees International Union). Third, as president of Lightstone Entertainment, I was instrumental in building the company and developing the project *3000 Miles to Graceland*, starring Kevin Costner and Kurt Russell.

Another shift was underway. As soon as I embodied the realization that when love drives our purpose, we are on course. That chapter of my life was complete.

That love moved me back home to North Carolina in 2004. I bought a condo there and flipped it. Struck by the simple success, I created a business relationship with an asset manager, who fed me listings. *Eller Your Home Seller* was born. I soon headed up a team of eleven focused on selling to flippers.

It was clear that I had reinvented myself. The fashion model—who was accustomed to doing what she was told—was completely replaced by the businesswoman who was there for other people. I was redesigning my life, and coaching others to redesign theirs.

Gary R. was the perfect partner. In 2011, Gary recruited me to work with him at Keller-Williams in Los Angeles. It was not as a real estate agent, but as a Productivity Coach for Keller-Williams in Studio City and the Hollywood Hills. For the next two years, I coached real estate agents on how to make their businesses successful by building teams. Gary and I shared a similar style, in that we always saw people's potential. When they saw themselves as glass-half-empty, we saw them as glass-half-full. We both also took a stand for their future possibilities in the face of their cynicism and resignation.

As a Productivity Coach, my formula was to pour love into them, so that they knew they had what it took to be successful. I trained them in structures, so they could track and manage their numbers that were embedded in programs, like lead generation, 36-12-3 (thirty-six sales in twelve months with three-hours of lead generation per day), buyer's consultation and listing presentations. These training sessions were built to create relationship-based transactions, resulting in referrals. I coached them to fall in love with their clients and to take care of them while building a respected name for themselves.

I moved up to CEO of the Keller-Williams in Marina Del Rey, coaching the top twenty-percent. As CEO, my goal was to empower everyone on the team. My job was to build careers worth having, businesses worth owning, lives worth living, experiences worth giving and legacies worth leaving.

People think that there must be some secret sauce. It includes commitment, integrity and fun. I trained them to be unreasonable, to commit to whatever they wanted to do and enjoy doing it. If you are committed, you are going to find a way to get it done. I just loved them up, lit them up and held them to account.

At this point, I realized that I was into my next shift. It was all about the training and the love of training, and the love that they could build a business that would last over time.

Another love presented itself, called family love. One of my nephews experienced a tough breakup with a girlfriend. I invited him to move in with me in L.A. I gratefully took him in. We lived together for eight years. It was a mother-son relationship, which was something I had always wanted.

But, if you asked him, he'd say, "She ain't my mama. She's my aunt. Aunt Donna."

All this time, I had been leading courses for thousands. These were courses that were designed to empower people and to encourage them to take on games in the world that would fulfill their lives' dreams and purpose. Their games live on. This is because, for the past sixteen years, I have collected participants' videos and created a mini-movie for these programs. You can view them at TeamLeadership.org. It is my project to have these peoples' passions produced and seen, so they are known and heard in the world. It brings that film piece of me into what I'm doing now.

The stories the participants create are astounding. For example, I once asked an elderly woman, "What are you up to, that you would want to do this video?"

She said, "I want to hold those addicted babies, until they stop crying. I've spent my whole nursing career walking past that window, and there was never a time when they were all at peace."

After she retired, at the age of seventy, she declared that she would have every one of those babies not cry, for at least one day. So, she returned to her old hospital, sitting with every single baby, until each one fell asleep. After the local media told her story, it went viral. A hospital, across the country, heard the story and hired her to create a program to train retired nurses on how to calm the addicted babies and put them to sleep.

I've shared this story many times, and given that she has just passed, telling her story is how I can keep her legacy alive. She made me cry, by how much she loved her babies.

I get moved to tears every time the participants share their projects with me and my team, when we ask them, "Why do you want your game to be videoed?"

One evening, a young man said from his wheelchair, "I love to surf, and I will surf again, even with one leg."

He tells us he was in his early twenties, when his leg was blown off in the Middle East. He loved to surf, and, when he came home, he wanted to return to surfing. He convinced a local surfboard company in San Diego to design surfboards for amputees. Now, he teaches them how to surf on these special surfboards, specifically designed for them. He calls his project Amped. The local news learned of the program, and his project, too, went viral.

Amazing ideas are born out of these games, like the young woman who calls her company Dykes with Drills. She is empowering women in the LGBTQ community to build tiny houses.

She says, "Why *can't* women use power tools, too?"

The common thread is my philosophy: *Love as a Way of Life*. It's probably no surprise then, that midway through these projects, I fell back in love with my childhood sweetheart. I was forty-three by then, and this was my first marriage. For me, it was unconditional love, and I was all about love, fun, excitement and self-expression.

The marriage lasted only three years. He presented me with a prenup (which I signed), as we walked into the wedding. As my mom puts it, *I had to marry him to divorce him*. In other words, it was to make way for the true love I would later find.

All our experiences help us to find out who we are. I am designing the love and the life I want to live. This is even more true now.

The man who will be my second husband, is a contractor in Detroit, president of MIG Construction. He builds casinos, apartment buildings and parking decks for a living. Ironically, that's what we have in common.

When we were dating, I said, "Wanna see one of my flips?"

And, he said, "Yes."

So, as I was showing him pictures of my flip, he said, "Did you take those walls down between the kitchen, living room and the dining room?"

And, I said, "Yeah, and I put that beam up, too."

And, he said, "You put a beam up?"

And, I said, "Yeah! I put a beam up!" And, in that moment, I fell in love.

Brian Deming and I are deliberately building a solid foundation together for our relationship. We are designing our marriage, so that it will last a lifetime. We get to say the way it's going to go.

Consistent with that, I am fearless when I'm coaching my clients to confront the unworkability of their lives.

People say to me, "I want want want want want."

I confront them, by saying that wanting something is meaningless, if there is no action. I say, "Take action! If you really want it, you'll go get it."

When I think back to that first shift, while I was still modeling, I could see that I kept reinventing myself. My hair was long blonde, short blonde, red, black, even bald. I played it edgy, and I evoked Princess Diana. At that time, I was also newly engaged in a personal and professional growth program. And, out of that training, I got that—above all—I was a businesswoman.

For one moment, before that transformation, I saw myself as an old, ugly, demeaning, pissed-off angry woman, because I lived out of wanting to be *right*. Suddenly, with that shift, I got that I am a beautiful woman. It was no longer necessary to keep playing with the twenty-year-olds. It was when I fell in love with myself again. It's when I turned my life around. It all shifted. I am not the same human being.

I coach my clients to take action. Wanting something makes no difference. *Do what you love*, I tell them. Make sure you're passionate about what you do, because you'll stay younger. The more you're feeding your soul with what is important to you, the more vibrant and alive and engaged you are. That's how I live. I'm timeless, I'm not sixty.

When I got that it's not about wanting to be right, I saw that it is about having love be the way that you live your life. I'm insistent that people around me are filled with their vibrancy, however that looks. *Choosing love, as a way of life*. This is because it is so invigorating, satisfying, fulfilling and rejuvenating. It feeds the soul. Love is what fearless looks like. I could stand there forever.

Donna Eller

That she was a beautiful blonde fashion model featured in *Vogue*, *Harper's Bazaar*, *Self* and other top women's magazines for twenty years, doesn't begin to tell Donna Eller's story. Donna has fearlessly taken on corrupt modeling agencies, flipped houses, produced movies, clothed Wall Street men and coached thousands of people into being their best selves. Donna has set the stage for others' transformation, by demonstrating how she fearlessly walks her own path.

Raised in a small farming town in North Carolina, Donna made her way to New York City shortly after graduating from Bauder College in Fort Lauderdale, Florida. Soon after, she was picked up by Click, a top modeling agency, and also modeled for IMG, Ford and Wilhelmina. She has also modeled internationally and acted in television commercials, ranging from Oil of Olay, Dove Soap, to Breyers Ice Cream.

Not just the proverbial pretty face, Donna was the co-founder of The Models' Guild, Local 51, in 1995. She served as its Union President for five years and lobbied for the protection of children's rights in the modeling industry.

That work garnered her notice on the *Today Show*, *20-20*, *60 Minutes*, *Hard Copy*, *New York One Minute*, *Good Morning America* and WCBS. This time, instead of her beauty being captured in images in print, it was her work that was featured in stories in *The New York Times*, *The New York Post*, *New York Magazine* and others.

Still in the entertainment industry, her career path took a turn to producing movies. She was President of Lightstone Entertainment.

Donna also was at the helm of Spirit Models, Vice President of Public Relations for The Haberdasher and a Business Consultant for VSA Consulting Group.

While her professional career blossomed, Donna also began working with Landmark Worldwide, a personal and professional training organization. Donna has nearly three decades of experience in Transformation and Training and Development. She is currently a Personal Performance Coach for Landmark, while also leading Communication Courses, as well as The Team, Management, and Leadership Program.

After her New York chapter, Donna headed back home and began flipping houses. Discovering she had a talent for real estate, Donna opened One Hot Flip. She built an award-winning Keller Williams team in North Carolina. It was then on to being CEO for Keller Williams Realty in Marina Del Rey and Rancho Palos Verdes in Los Angeles, California, as well as being a realtor and a productivity coach.

Led by her love and passion for bringing out the best in herself and others, Donna devotes herself to empowering others in leadership, performance and team building.

Donna Eller
Personal Performance Coach
Donna@DonnaEller.com
www.DonnaEller.com

Taylor Leigh Cannizzaro

Becoming Leadership in Action

Saying YES!

...to create, to call you into being and to open up something previously unrealized.

One sunny afternoon in Encinitas, CA, I met a woman working alongside her boss at a coffee shop. Through our conversation, he invited me to wakesurf. "To what?", I said. He chuckled and said, 'To wakesurf. It's like surfing but behind a boat, it is kind of like water skiing without the rope" Despite having tried none of these sports, I said yes! I went with them not too long after and little did I know that day would forever change the direction of my life. Learning something completely out of my comfort zone created novel paths in my way of thinking. Every time I go, it's a new experience and challenge: trying a new board, trick or way of riding. After continuing to show up consistently and on time, I developed a community and family of wakesurfers. We are a tribe that loves each other and supports the growth of one another. I cherish the moments and days on the water as opportunities to let go, be free, relax and be creative.

Challenges are opportunities to increase your confidence and demonstrate that you can do something you don't know how to initially do. Step outside of your comfort zone: who you know yourself to be and what you think you're capable of doing. This creates an opening of power, magic, and opportunity in other areas of life. For me, wakesurfing and later surfing became access to a new way of viewing and approaching life.

Life was fine at the time: I drove a nice car. I was fit, attractive and generally happy. Nothing to see here and everyone thought I was happy. Actually, I was dying inside. I felt an immense, unrealized potential pulsing to be unleashed. There was a burning desire and I didn't know how, I didn't know what, I just knew I had to do something different than what I was doing. I needed to try something new. Within every person, there is a leader with a passion and commitment waiting to be self-expressed, fulfilled, and understood.

Whatever you can imagine, question or think of that lights you up and gets you moving, that is your opportunity lottery ticket!

- What matters most to you?
- What is the next vision you would really like to jump into fulfilling?
- What would you like to grow and develop in?
- What is important to you?

Developing the *'Selfware'*

...of the mind to shift your experience.

The world around us is a direct reflection of the occurrences and thoughts in our own minds. What exists was first spoken into existence. Everything exists because we said so. We get to choose. That is the power of what's between our two ears bringing into existence what we think and then speak into existence. We create what we think. We create what we think we are capable of and worthy of. Upgrading the programming and becoming *selfware* shifts the experience of life.

Life does not occur as it is. It occurs as who we are. 'Occurred' is defined as something that happened, took place, existed or was found, or it is a thought or idea coming into someone's mind. It is a function of perception. What we perceive is a function of our thoughts, feelings, considerations, and opinions fueled by our previous experiences. With that in mind, ask yourself for any situation, at any time, "How is this person occurring to me right now? How does a situation occur to me? How is an experience occurring?" Consider how something occurs may or may not be the truth. Have you ever heard: 'Don't believe everything you think?" There is how the world is and how the world occurs to us.

We have the ability to understand how something occurs for us, shift the context and make a choice. We do have a say in the matter. This takes practice and is a journey in becoming self-aware. Thus this is developing your *selfware*. However, if left to our own devices, we will fall into old programming. It's only natural. The machinery kicks in, the story takes off and the world is painted a certain way based on past experiences.

When we can develop our *selfware*, then the way something and the world occurs transforms. We become.

What if you can choose a new set of colors? What if you could create a new picture of what your life is like, because you say so. This is the magic. This is the opportunity of creation. Did you know that creation and reaction are the same letters rearranged? In a time of creation, you say so, you choose, you are the one who gets to paint from the present moment, put a stroke here, place another there, fill in the colors or leave it empty. In a time of reaction, there is an auto-pilot taking over the paint strokes and the colors flood in determined by previous experiences and associations.

Since my youth, I've been fiercely curious about reading books, taking seminars and attending classes. We are our greatest investment. When I put curiosity into action in the world, I gained access to an understanding, practice, and realization of how to become.

To become means, 'to start to be'. Consider this as the journey of becoming. Then what is it to be? To exist, to be alive, to come about, to arise, to happen, to take place to have existence, to have life, to transpire, to occur… It's who I always have been, it's who you always have been…it's who we ARE right now. It's a function of realizing who you are free from any constraints.

At first, I didn't understand that I actually had so much power. In fact, we all don't. Inside of all of us is a leader waiting to be released. Removing the veils of my perceptions and believing I had that much power with consistency, is, was and continues to be the greatest feat of all. I cannot tell you how many times, I take a deep breath, give up and realize: it is not necessarily so. It's a practice of awareness and developing the *selfware* to upgrade the operating system of the mind.

Collective Uplift

...We are as boats in a harbor, when they rise...we rise together!—Taylor Leigh Cannizzaro

Surround yourself with people that pull you into your greatness. Create an environment where you are self-expressed, free and inspired. Provide a space for people to gather together and reveal the power in every human.

Henry Ford once said, "If everyone is moving forward together, then success takes care of itself."

Embracing the Journey

...Happiness is letting go of the outcome.—Taylor Leigh Cannizzaro

Standing in and being with, is a concept that has led me down many beautiful paths.

As a teenager, my aunt was diagnosed with cancer. My aunt Phil was and is the matriarch of my family, as I know it. After my sophomore year in high school, my mom sent me to live with my aunt for the summer. I was studying nutrition, yoga, personal development, communication, and spirituality. We spent the summer sharing and laughing. I also taught her about everything I was learning. This involved consciousness and attitude and a specialized Japanese way of eating and living called Macrobiotics.

She began shifting the way she engaged with the world and the way she ate. The doctors had told her that she had just six months to live. Over time, that six-month date passed and she was continuing to live. Two years later, I went to live at the Kushi Institute in Massachusetts. I cooked in exchange for my room and board, taught classes for others. These people were dealing with life-threatening, degenerative diseases, where Western medicine had told them that they couldn't help them anymore.

That's when I really got it. It wasn't about me anymore. I became of service to other people. I created a plan to alleviate the suffering from cancer and disease. My whole life became focused around people's health and nutrition. I became a molecular biologist. I worked for the diagnosis, prognosis, and treatment of cancer. I worked in laboratories. I became a consultant and began launching new tests to market, validating and developing quality control systems and standard operating procedures. I then started working at startups, where we launched companies from scratch. We were always forwarding personalized medicine: how can we create a more effective and intelligent treatment strategy killing the cancer, without as much toxicity to the patient.

After reaching a certain point, though, it wasn't fulfilling. I always had a vision of being out in the world. I was behind the lab bench, swamped launching a startup, experiencing personal frustration, lacking expression of the potential that I knew I had inside. I didn't know what was needed in order to realize it. I started doing transformational and leadership training with an organization called Landmark. In 2016, I completed my first course, which began as a weekend. In the third course, the program has the participants take on a project. The leader asked, "What are you passionate about? What impact would you like to see in the world that isn't occurring now?" Previously unmanaged thoughts of not being good enough, not being capable and a persistent fear of failure would come rushing in. Now, my mind was freed up to create and explore.

Being Committed

...creates an unstoppable you.

Commitment and consistency are everything. The following passage is so important that I'm including it here. I have returned to it often over the years. It captures the essence of the practice required to fulfill what matters the most to you...to fulfill the expression of your passion and purpose.

"Until one is committed, there is hesitancy, the chance to draw back, always ineffectiveness. Concerning all acts of initiative and creation, there is one elementary truth the ignorance of which kills countless ideas and splendid plans: that the moment one definitely commits oneself, then providence moves too.

All sorts of things occur to help one that would never otherwise have occurred. A whole stream of events issues from the decision, raising in one's favour all manner of unforeseen incidents, meetings and material assistance which no man could have dreamed would have come his way.

Whatever you can do or dream you can, begin it. Boldness has genius, power and magic in it. Begin it now."—J.W. Goethe

After living in San Diego for five years, I finally ocean surfed in Nicaragua! Friends and colleagues said they'd take me out. However, without the commitment of time together, a board and a wetsuit; it just never happened. Then, my friend invited me to come with her to Nicaragua, while she sold her house there. Every time she went, she hired a gentleman to take her out. I was very excited after all this time talking about it, yet I was nervous since I had been told that it was difficult (ahem, fear of failure). After almost two hours, I came back to shore exhausted, exhilarated and with a huge smile on my face (I did what I did not think I would be capable of).

When I returned home, I declared that upon borrowing a board and wetsuit from a friend, if I went consistently, then and only then would I purchase my own equipment. After 30 days of going consistently, I bought my gear. I've been hit a few times with a board (whether my own or someone else's). Once while wakesurfing, the board hit me in the lip after attempting a 360, seven stitches later. Then it happened another time while ocean surfing, three stitches later. My friends had asked me after each instance, if that would be the last time. The only thing I could think I was, 'Bummer, I'll have to stay out of the water until I heal!!' It's now been five years since I first ocean surfed. Today, the only thing preventing me from surfing daily is business travel.

I simply love the ocean and getting out there. I'm not amazing, nor perfect. I remember apologizing to an older gentleman thinking I was in his way. He replied, "Darling, I've been surfing for fifty years, and I'm still learning." I'm committed to trying with a willingness to want to, that embraces the challenge while listening to myself, when the ocean is strong and fierce.

Finding Connection

...immersing yourself shifts perception and awareness to open oneself to what is important to you.

As an avid hiker in Colorado mountains and a surfer (both behind the boat and out at sea), a practitioner of yoga and a fitness junkie. I seek connection to nature and the sensation of being alive.

Surfing in the ocean gives me a tangible enjoyment. I feel the water, the waves, the wind, the colors in the sky and upon the water, the sun, the rain when it comes and the feeling of *all* of it. There is a sensation of deep connection with the experience of being *in* the ocean, which has proven different for me than stand up paddling. When I ocean surf, I experience immersion and a presence that is absolutely breathtaking. Many times, I come in from surfing feeling like a drowned animal, exhausted and still with a huge smile on my face. I feel elated with fulfillment, peace and a sense of contentment. There's also the added bonus of feeling like I just got everything out of my system... anything that is stuck, residual and unspoken.

Allowing Creativity

...for realizations, making it up as you go!!!

Sitting on my board off the beaches of Encinitas, California, I was looking out into the horizon, thinking and halfway meditating when a piece of plastic floated by. As an oncological molecular biologist, I visualized plastic photodegradation in the ocean. At that moment, I could understand the visceral impact of pervasive microplastics as molecules everywhere in everything. There are 100 million animals that die from plastics every year.

The very plastic that killed is released to kill again and again. Polluting the oceans is catastrophic. Our very own survival is linked to the survival of ocean ecosystems. The gravity hit me, as the magnitude washed over me. My focus has always been people's health and now I realized that the ocean's health is just, if not, more important. Stopping ocean plastic pollution became a new passion and purpose.

Remember the third transformational learning course, when I was asked to take on a project? I chose to help people reduce their single-use plastic footprint. But how? It began as a desire and a will, and generated into a conversation. "OK then, how do I start this as a conversation?" I wondered. "What does that look like?" By asking questions and talking to people in San Diego and Encinitas, I attended an Encinitas city council meeting focused on the topic of banning expanded polystyrene foam (EPS) aka. Styrofoam™. While I was there, I met the San Diego Surfrider Foundation team. The current Chair of the Rise Above Plastics committee had recently stepped down. It wasn't long before their Program Coordinator said, "You seem passionate. You have a lot of energy. Do you want to take on being the Chair of the Rise Above Plastics Committee?" I looked at him and said, "What does that mean?" Being willing to explore what it meant, having no idea and with a few follow up conversations, I accepted the opportunity. I had no idea what I was going to be doing or what the responsibility would be.

That's how my ocean advocacy began; by saying YES!! My ocean advocacy began by surfing, allowing myself to be connected to nature and inspired to take action after being freed up by the constraints of my mind. By continuing to have conversations and asking questions, holding meetings and doing research we decided to launch a 'Plastic Straws Suck' campaign. Then we released a 'Fight the Foam' campaign. We hosted events, movie screenings, and rallies. Working with local politicians, we were able to shift policy and ban Styrofoam™ in all of San Diego. That is how I became a local advocate in San Diego.

Creating a Sense of Urgency

The Earth is in the midst of a mass life extinction. Humans are at the center influencing this great environmental degradation and what is called the new Anthropocene epoch. Scientists estimate that 150-200 species become extinct every 24 hours. This is nearly 1,000 times the "natural" or "background" rate and, many biologists say that is greater than anything the world has experienced, since the vanishing of the dinosaurs nearly 65 million years ago.

There I was, standing at SeaWorld, behind the scenes with the dolphins. I watched the two sweet little girls I had brought, as they delighted in the experience. We were so close!! My heart broke as I watched the dolphins in captivity thinking about what we are doing to the oceans, their homes, and countless other innocent sea creatures. One dolphin then swam back and forth at hip level, with one eye peering straight into me garnering my attention. I just stood there, astonished. The tears came. I felt a feeling of deep sorrow. As Chair of Surfrider Foundation's Rise Above Plastics, I was trying to make a difference and yet I knew it was too little, too late. I said, "I'm sorry, I want to do more and I don't know how!" The dolphin seemed to look back at me, as if to say, "Thank you, I know."

During that time, I was working on an online business, consulting as a scientist, volunteering as an ocean advocate and participating in a rigorous two year: Team, Management, and Leadership program. I love working on multiple projects with passion. My friends and family were on me to stop doing so much. They all said I had to stop the volunteerism. I felt that would be killing off a portion of myself. I was searching for answers and direction, while trusting the process, the journey and continuing to give up. I knew that money was tight. I was overwhelmed. I didn't know what I was doing and, sometimes, I was really confused.

The experience with the dolphin strengthened my conviction to continue my ocean advocacy. I knew I couldn't stop. It was a part of me. I also knew that I was on purpose and in action in a unique way. There was something about my efforts to stop ocean plastic that kept opening doors and moving forward. It was bigger than me. All I knew was that I had to just keep taking steps in that direction and literally just trying different things and not knowing how it was supposed to look or be.

In the next few months, David Katz from Plastic Bank contacted me and said, "I think it's time for you to join Plastic Bank and our global organization." I laughed and said, "What would that look like?" After a few months of discussion, I joined the Plastic Bank team in Vancouver, BC for their global summit week. I got the world of what's possible in Plastic Bank and the impact that they're having alleviating poverty and stopping ocean plastic in Haiti, the Philippines, Indonesia, and Brazil.

Over 80% of ocean plastic comes from areas of extreme poverty. Imagine living under one dollar a day in an environment where you are uncertain if you will be able to feed your children. You live in a make-shift structure with no floor, no power and your children could die from the common fever. Would recycling be in your realm of comprehension? In areas of no proper waste management, the rivers and canals collect the material in the dry season. During the rainy season, all the waste rushes into the oceans. The average is a truckload of plastic entering the ocean every minute of every day...of every week...of every month...and every year!!!

Plastic Bank empowers disenfranchised communities to exchange plastic for currency. By enabling the exchange of plastic packaging for the things people need and cannot afford like school tuition, cooking fuel, WiFi, cell phone minutes, money or blockchain-secured digital tokens, Plastic Bank reveals the true value of the material, making it too valuable to throw away. Social Plastic® Ecosystems are creating the supply chain and the circular economy of all materials.

I had just launched a new genetics company detecting the predisposition of prostate cancer. All of a sudden, here I am in Vancouver completely enrolled in the vision of a global stand alleviating poverty and fighting ocean plastic. By the end of the week, David looked at me and said, "Yeah, we're not letting you go back to San Diego, without signing an agreement." I said, "Okay, let's explore what that could look like." We negotiated with the president and David as CEO and founder that Friday, after the week together. We signed the contract, and I started less than a month later. It was all because I said so. I stood in the possibility of creating a new future giving up all notions of being good enough, doing it right, having to have it look a certain way. At least in that moment!!!!

Transforming from a local, San Diego ocean advocate to being a global leader, was not an easy transition. It's still not today. I am confronted on a daily basis. My ego identity challenges me: who I think I am, what I think I am capable as I step into greater heights of performance. In the first month of being with Plastic Bank, I cried and was confronted by having calls with the leadership teams of some of the biggest multinational companies around the world. I felt like I wasn't good enough, qualified or capable of having these conversations and/or creating these programs. It really was my identity and or my ego that wanted to take me out and not have me participate as a protection to stay safe and small.

A year later, I am a global executive developing relationships, programs and impact to engage people in Europe, Canada, and the U.S. as ambassadors. I unleash people's leadership and purpose in action, as we turn plastic into currency. The circular economy of materials places the value into the hands of the world's most impoverished people.

We are launching engagement programs for everyone to participate. Everyone wants to stop plastic pollution. We have created the opportunity for everyone to be in action and stewardship over the people and the oceans as we gather together and collectively uplift, anything is possible.

I empower people like you, and all of us, here in the United States, Canada and Europe, to fulfill a sense of purpose, and a sense of wanting to do something about what's happening in the ocean and about what's happening with the world's most impoverished communities. I create the programming and the bridge to taking action together. Plastic Bank began with a focus on building business relationships to create the infrastructure and ecosystems where we operate, where plastic pollution is occurring. For the first time, we are developing new programming together with people around the world to participate in our ecosystems.

Your local action and participation can create not only local impact but also global impact, to further prevent plastic from entering the ocean. We are engaging the staff of the multinational companies around the world (involving millions of people) as we develop our Impact Ambassador programming and curriculums. Every workplace, school and congregation can now become a part of our ecosystem to alleviate poverty and stop ocean plastic. We are gathering together to create a connection for the transformation and economic development of all stakeholders. For example, a student in New York could be connected to a student in Haiti, and be able to connect and understand how they're actually making a difference across continents.

Thank you for creating the opportunity of creating me, creating you!

Together, we become the people to effect the change we want to see in the world.

Welcome Home

In that breaking moment.
It's the roaring ocean's unrest, not far from your own...
You carefully watch for the ideal wave.
You see one, and you can't let it go.
It's perfect for you.
The wind on your face.
Uncertain of what will happen.
You launch yourself into it, unleashing yourself into the world.

—Taylor Leigh Cannizzaro

Taylor Leigh Cannizzaro

Taylor Leigh Cannizzaro is Chief Alliance Officer at Plastic Bank, speaker, author, and mentor. She unleashes people's leadership and purpose in action. Turning plastic and trash into currency for the circular economy of materials, Plastic Bank places the value into the hands of the world's most impoverished people. Taylor identifies and develops potential opportunities to deliver value and impact through partner alliances and the application of assets. Her systems strategy has launched companies, programs and campaigns. She has also integrated policy into governmental action. She's hosted events, emceed, led seminars and keynote engagements. She has also built and led teams. Her background as a molecular-oncology scientist, certified health coach, and yoga instructor, combined with her leadership, management, and team-building skills, allows her to take the most complex situations and offer simple solutions and results.

Taylor enjoys hitting the gym, practicing yoga, ocean surfing, and wake surfing. Her highly personable, enthusiastic and uplifting personality makes connecting with her extremely easy. It's her passion for the health of people and the oceans worldwide that powers her drive.

Taylor Leigh Cannizzaro
Plastic Bank
619-818-5150
Taylor@PlasticBank.com
www.ResponsibleGreenLiving.com

Kimberly Genovese

Broken & Shattered to Magnificent Stained Glass

Living Fearlessly—oh, the Glory of it all—and what a ride it has been to be here in a life that has overcome Mediocrity and embraced a context of Fearlessness. Did you know we are all born with fearlessness? Fear is learned, dare we say acquired through communication. Being Fearful or having Fear in and of itself is not the concern. It is quite the opposite. Wouldn't you agree that having access to Fear can be quite beneficial? Fear of death can insight someone to quit life-long habits overnight. Fear of failure can cause someone to get support to be successful. Fear, of itself, is a powerful tool. Where we can go horribly off track, is if we embrace Fear as a context to live out our lives. THAT is where deep darkness can arrive, penetrate the cells of your Being and never depart. The result—at best—is a sense of lukewarm living. No matter how outrageously successful we are—there is always this sense that something is missing, a sense of falling short or being unfulfilled or a sense of being empty. [That common conversation where everyone tells you how lucky you are—or how they wish they had what you have, and you think to yourself even every so slightly: Yeah, but…] At worse, tragically, well, let's just say dying with our Music still in us, our authentic Magnificence never released and Our unique Gifts never shared. Inasmuch as I am someone who has gone to those deep tragic dark places and almost took my life, I THANK GOD and The Angels for my Life's Mission and Purpose never allowing for me to let it all end there or I promise you this Fearless Story would never have been written.

Are you curious to hear what that Mission and Purpose is that pulled for my Fearlessness? Here it is: "Set ALL LIFE Free; Lead the Way to Celebrate ALL LIFE and have ALL LIFE live harmoniously together."

This Calling was verbally given to me as early as the age of four. I state this now for you here for two purposes:

1. I will refer to it in my Story

2. To be clear on what your Life's Mission and Purpose is CRITICAL in the realm of living your best life. I give this to you now for it is not only quite glorious and peaceful to be present to being on course and having a North Star to guide you; it will—literally—pull you forth to living a Fearless Life.

Here Is My Journey from Mediocrity to Fearlessness...

My Mom, Aunt and Grandmother let me know that I came out of the womb, literally, a bright light—dancing and singing and just emulating all that is pure joy and love. It started slow—the conversation of fear—it started as simple as being told to "contain" my enthusiasm not be quite so electric. Then at the age of two, the Big D entered my life. Divorce. Burned into my brain were my father's words: "I don't love you, I never did—get out of my house." Whether they are the exact and accurate words, I do not know and to this day; that is what I heard. Devasted, living inside of my Dad's words and kicked out of the only home I had known up until then, I got my first taste of abandonment and I will tell you as someone who's love language is touch and words of acknowledgment (Five Love Languages) that was devastatingly scary for me.

Now, up until two, aside from the "contain yourself" I was pretty free to BE child-like awe, wonder and curiosity. The best that childhood has to offer us! You know—that giddy sensation waking up every day exuberant about today's adventure. Jumping up and down begging to take on the day. That ability to get up on a giant horse and ride it without any sense of fear—just pure joy! Or to take a mountain in Colorado that adults would shiver at the thought of skiing and you can't get up there fast enough. The kind of fearlessness that we all warm up on the inside watching children exhibit and long for those days of seemingly reckless abandon.

Well, it was the blow with Divorce, then living in multiple households (my parents married and divorced multiple times and I would live in the different homes) where fear really came to live with me in ways I could not have seen coming. What I am pointing to is abuse. Mostly verbal, some physical and slight sexual was all intertwined over the next decade. There were many many dark days in my childhood—locked in dark basements and closets by step-parents, introduced to dark spirits, chased by a whole school full of children—I met fear face-on to the point of becoming petrified. Petrified to the point of being frozen in place—think of a petrified tree. Presented with life-threatening situations; I would count myself triumphant to live another day and survive the darkness—not noticing that I was stuck in place—no longer being a fearless Evil Knievel daredevil exhilarated to take on the next new great adventure of that day. Not noticing that my slippery slope from radical ridiculous accomplishments and being a trailblazer to rooting myself in being a petrified tree; deeply rooted and stuck surviving as an existence instead. Now, don't get me wrong—living another day in an environment where you believe you are in jeopardy of being killed—true or not—is a huge accomplishment. So, the lukewarm living begins…the mediocrity creeps in—just notice—take advantage of noticing it. I didn't get to do that then, so please you see it now, for yourself and reap the rewards. Just look and see the layering of the existence with FEAR. Existing with FEAR stole my bountiful prosperous existence to get to cause all life to be celebrated and enjoyed… and created a mediocre life of "making it through another day"; completely off-course and in the seas of mediocrity.

You see, I was blessed, blessed beyond measure to meet Jesus at the very young age of four. It was not the way most might think. You see, it took a woman who was married to my Father who called herself a Witch and did witch-craft while my Father was away at work and she would use me in her rituals. This not only created an environment where Jesus could show up and shine a bright light on me, it also created an environment for me to meet Dark Spirits—when she would lock me in the damp, cold basement with the lights out—this, also unknowingly at the time was to be a great blessing beyond measure to meet Dark Spirits that I would like to stop and point out for you. THIS is where, I did not know it at the time—EVERYTHING, I mean everything is available to be used to move you into being FEARLESS vs FEARFUL. Everything— especially those that look like they are not. TAKE ADVANTAGE of my Story and choose the path of Fearlessness NOW. It will have you reap great rewards in record time!!

For Me Though and My Story—Enter Fear, Again, at the Level of Being Petrified…

Now, believing in the Darkness—by the light of day—I was quite free. Quite free indeed. Now, I bring this to you as it—again – insidiously so—began to create a routine, then a habit to be someone who survives the Evenings of a day, as opposed to thrives in them. I remind you this is insidious—like a lobster being put into a pot of cold water and then turned to a boil—you cannot feel the hands of mediocrity strangling you and bottling you, until well after you have become extremely comfortable in the environment. Stealing my nights—that is at a minimum 25% of a day!!! We are talking about priceless lost hours!!! Imagine what one might do with all those hours?

So, fast forward, along with dark destructive people I was introduced to in my childhood, I've also received wonderful, magical ones. Enter Jan Gleason. Jan married my Father and they owned a horse farm where they breed Appaloosas, had five Afghan dogs and Jan was training to be in the Olympics as an equestrian competitor. The imprinting placed on my heart to celebrate that would reconstruct and insure that I would never quit. THANK YOU GOD. You see say hello to the power and magic of Nature, animals, love and fertile soil. You see, just as rich—yes, you heard me—just as rich as the experience of the Black Magic Witch my Father introduced me to—he also introduced me to the Magical gift of a woman who had been raised in a very rich and productive environment. Who by the grace of my Mother and my Father—I was allowed to learn from for a period of 7th to 9th grade of school. Between my time with nature, the horses, the dogs—the garden, oh the glorious garden and being guardian by Jan, I re-accessed my child-like awe, wonder and curiosity. I broke completely free from the shackles of fear. Truly, I was back to a fearless—joy-filled living. Nothing seemed impossible. The awareness that who I am is a Fairy from a magical land; little did I know that it would be set into me with such a deep profound purpose…

You see my Mom married a wonderful man—the man of her dreams, her Knight in shining armor and we moved into a beautiful home built by both my Mom and Mike. She was so excited to give me this Gift. He even adopted me legally to make me feel that I was finally given a home—a whole and complete family and home. So wonderful. So gracious. So loving. Yet Darkness flooded over me and took hold. I could not see the precious gift they were giving me. I did not want to live in this home. I wanted to go back to the Horse Farm. I felt that I had been stripped of the magical land and future that was given to me, so I was BACK. Back in a state of having a glorious home taken from me which took me back to Fear.

I had mastered the Art of Fear to the level of petrified as you may recall; add rage-filled. A lethal cocktail. At this point I am in high school, now just imagine—back in school with people I met in grade school and yet I didn't know them and they didn't know me. I was a fish out of water gasping for breath, until I met my high school sweetheart. He appeared to be a gem and don't misunderstand me, he was. We just never had a shot. You see, I lost my virginity to this young man and with it—yes, the very first time—I got pregnant. What a mess!! My Mom is finally happy with the Man of Her Dreams and I am pregnant. Keep in mind I am also humming inside a context of petrified and rageful. The cocktail is now complete.

AGAIN, HEED MY STORY—Inside all this fear, rage and confusion came the beginning of my end. I sealed my future of mediocrity, by being so fearful of how telling my Mother that I was pregnant would devastate her and literally would result in the end of my life—I opted at the direction of my friends—to get an abortion. Now it is critical that you understand something here. Remember my Life's Purpose? To Celebrate ALL LIFE and have ALL LIFE live harmoniously together…this broke that calling at the highest level—at the tippy top of that mountain. My life of living fearfully and petrified had hit its lowest low of which I might never return. I became—immediately—shattered and forever broken. Hateful and abusive to myself to the point of becoming suicidal. I am 17 years old. Just get it. 17 years old. Due to the conversation of fear being so real for me, it could have taken me out as early as the age of 17.

Side note: You know I have to laugh as I type these next words for you; if it wasn't for the requirement to earn a living to pay the bills, I might not be here today to share this story. You see, I had to work. I had to earn a living. If it was not for the GRACE of others' appreciation and the restating of my value at/through my employment every single day, I may have been successful in taking myself out.

The reason I bellowed early in laughter is—at the time—I had channeled a good portion of my rage toward money. I blamed money for most of my ills. It is so great to come full circle back to not only being fearless again, being able to see all the good that is available when you have money as a resource. Give up duality. Most everything is not purely good or purely evil; it just isn't.

OK, back to the story…not only did my most intimate and loving relationships to date come from either being employed or being an entrepreneur—my most radical and prosperous accomplishments have as well. TRIUMPHANT! Yes and No. You see, everything I mean everything in my life was now being built on top of petrified and rage. Really. Have you ever heard that context is decisive? Well, it is!

Little did I know, this would be the Cornerstone on which my Kingdom would be built. So, there I was, graduating from High School, seemingly the whole world before me and back to being someone who was just getting through each day without quitting on myself...this is an interesting part to the story. Due to the incredible response to who I was in my jobs (constant high accolades, salaries and promotion) there was just enough to keep me engaged at a very high level. I became a receptionist at a law firm at the age of 18, within two weeks was promoted to a docket clerk and within six months sent to paralegal school. I was one of the first paralegals in Chicago and also one of the highest-paid. Now, stop and notice—again, I am building success and accomplishment on top of fear. FEAR of being discovered for the monster that I was. A mother who would kill her own child. BE CLEAR: I did not and I do not think this of anyone who has had an abortion. ONLY ME. I was living inside of knowing myself as the most horrible human on the planet. I mean worse than Hitler, Dahmer and John Wayne Gacy all rolled up into one human. I had "seemingly" great accomplishments. Accomplishments people would love to have and yet they were actually mediocre for what I was capable of and lack-luster.

This is where you want to take a special note from my story. WHO you surround yourself with MATTERS. My next set of guardian angels to enter my life were: my best friend of 35+ years came from my employment, as did my White Knight—my husband of 27 years. Both of which when it came to that devasting day in our relationships, that I would share my abortion with them, knowing they would excommunicate me forever and did not. This is when my journey from the darkness back into the light began. I shared with Pam, my best friend, and then with my husband and Rock, Steve; neither cared. Not one bit!! Not at all!! What?!? How could this be?!? This makes NO SENSE. The road to fearless living on the path of forgiveness and redemption began. I had it ALL! Great husband, Great friends, Great home, Great Life!

Know this is where you really want to sit on the edge of your chair and hear me: you can build a SEEMINGLY FULL and MIRACULOUS, potentially envious life—you can!!! And you will never know that the thief of FEAR has stolen your Music, your Magnificence, your Gifts—TRUST ME, you won't even know. You will think everything is fine and dandy—you have a great life—and you do! If it wasn't for God's call in the middle of the night to have more money come in the front door then we can shovel out the back door—for underneath it all I had a HUGE FEAR of money and it's ills and the built-in, now low-grade, if even apparent petrified fear and rage would raise it's head again now through this pathway called wealth.

My husband and I may have kept walking further and further down the bunny trail of mediocrity and quiet despair without realizing it—ever maybe. Until we did. Again, be thankful always for what appears to be destructive to you. THE KEYS to the KINGDOM are to experience them through a FEARLESSNESS vs. a FEARFULNESS. Learn from us, so that you can save yourself precious time and needless anguish. Say hello to the crash of 2008. Everything my husband and I had built began to erode. FEAR reared it's ugly head yet again and brought with it rage and mediocrity; now almost to the point of bankruptcy, literally.

It was not until we experienced a glorious 3 ½ day Program that we could actually catch and see the damage done by living a life filled and suppressed with fear. You see up until then, we thought it was awesome to be courageous and brave. And please do not misunderstand me. Just like Fear; Courage and Bravery are key tools to have in your toolbox.

They Are Not a Way to Live Your Life…

You see I had been living my life since 17 as a Survivor. A Martyr. Grateful to be alive and indulgent in the fear of being exposed for being a Monster—surviving and martyring is not the most powerful ways to bring about Celebration, Harmony and Joy. Trust me. I know. Especially if they are derived on top of being Unworthy and fear of being found Unworthy.

So from the age of 49-54, I dove deep into the Art and Mastery of Being Agape Love, Illuminating Light, a Servant Leader and a Purpose-filled Philanthropic and what a ride it has been. About halfway through my six-year journey—your gonna love this—I got just how hard and exhausting it is to be constantly courageous…that it was this day the ground underneath me altered; I still shake my head when I state that reality. Once I walked right into this reality, I never looked back! It would be nice to be able to say that at that moment everything shifted and I have never been fearful again. Well, in some ways it did. I was most definitely emptied of the decades of it. It definitely did. I mean—once you get that fearless is easier than courageous, there is no turning back. There just isn't.

That being said, I had built decades of darkness on top of my Brilliant Hope Diamond—that each and every one of us is—and that dark "Coal" wasn't in any hurry of moving on. So, in many ways, everything changed that day and my life immediately shifted—and for anyone who has seen the movie the Secret Garden—it takes time and loving effort before the New Garden fully appears. For me, about three years for full manifestation. Over three decades to get there and three years to blossom back—now that three years doesn't seem so long, does it? (Giant smile)

My Life is no longer mediocre—not even close and I am thrilled to report the petrified fear, rage and mediocrity are gone! I am a glorious child of God living a life full and free. I spend each and every day 100% engaged in my Life's Purpose and Mission and having it all—and not just for me!!! For ALL LIFE!! My Spirit, Body and Mind operate as One Entity. My marriage is thriving. My joy is in every moment of every day and I am ravenous to live life every moment as child-like awe, wonder and curiosity vs fear, rage and doubt. I will settle for nothing less than a life filled with breaking records and making history and every moment filled with joy, love, fun/playfulness and peace.

The gift I offer you and invite you to take is to look. Just look. Where ever you are present to a lack of fulfillment or mediocrity; I promise you some form of fear is present. Do what it takes to remove that fear, until you are present to being without fear; fearless.

Good news. Bad news…mediocrity has its hold on all of us. Since I have had the treasure to be released of my dark, deep, debilitating levels of fear, I have had the incredible luxury to work with—side by side—Global leaders; be very very clear: fear, rage, doubt run ramped in humanity and it never "ends," regardless of how high you climb.

Be a Warrior. A Warrior expanding your Territory in and with communication with Others. What do I mean by all this? Trust, Listen, Speak and Live as a Warrior.

1. Pick the Spirit from which you manifest and TRUST YOURSELF and your choice!! God has always been present with me. What He looks like to me is Jesus. That is just how He has always shown Himself to me. I believe whole-heartedly God is Love and Love is everywhere. My Bible states the greatest commandment is to love God and love each other. Pick the version of God that is Love to you and run with it. I promise, Your Path is perfect. The sooner you trust your version of God (be it Jesus, Buddha, Dao, et al.) and move with Him; the sooner you will manifest a life of unbelievable outrageous accomplishments, for which mediocrity cannot even consider to meet you.

2. Create a Listening. What I mean by this is surround yourself with people, animals and/or nature who listen for your Greatness; not YES people and definitely not NO people. People who love you, care for you and are standing for your best life NOW. Who will listen to you beyond who you even see yourself to be! Think Champion. Who will champion you forward—no matter what—especially for when you won't champion yourself. This is critical; I am NOT pointing to advisors; especially those who have not gone where you are headed. One of the first of these is YOU! The faster you trust YOU/Intuition the better; then have ideally two others all listening/creating together with you in person, live video feed or by phone. These create the richest results. Communication is so much more than words—words alone are one dimensional.

3. Endurance; never, I mean, never quit. HEAR ME; yes I mean always be expanding—what I am most pointing to though, is HARMONY. Create a Spirit, Body, Mind harmony that allows for you to create an environment that will allow you to endure endlessly at the highest levels and building every day on top of the other as THE GREATEST DAY EVER.

My request for everyone—waste NO time. Stay diligent. Stay on Path. Awake every day in the JOY and PLEASURE that THIS LIFE RIGHT NOW is. When This Life is done. It is done. We have NO guarantees of what lies beyond this One. Live Fully...NOW. Waking up to realize the Devil stole what mattered most. Time—will be your greatest regret—Just look. Look at something that happened, let's say five years ago that at the time you thought was devasting and now it is just a bleep on the radar...just a bleep. Be present. Do not let current circumstances "take you out".

Here is to Your Fearless Radiantly Free Wealth-Being! Balance, Harmony...Dance, Sing—Let it all out—leave not one drop of your Greatness inside you. If you are breathing—NOW is your Time. I invite you to BE a Celebration of You and Life, now and now and now! I pray you take my Invitations, follow me and BOLT into your Story—that YOU write vs one being generated by fear/mediocrity. All love to you and yours!

Curious about what it is to be a Wealth-Being? Contact me. I'd love to share!! All Dreams are wired to lead you on Your Path. They are meant to exist, here, in reality—through you. Truly.

Anything is possible. Anything. Live Fearlessly. There may be no thing greater than *all life* treasured, celebrated and well-loved. Start with yours, now. That is my Dream. Join my Dream!

Kimberly Genovese

Kimberly is currently focused on the art of serial entrepreneurship. Her ability to provide fertile space for radical accomplishments is unprecedented. She has spent her life obsessed with being not just a difference. She is not satisfied until the difference for all is achieved, including mastering the art of creating consistent, reliable, miraculous results through authentic self-expression with freedom, ease and love present. In every new company she establishes, she is committed to being the gateway for the highest valuing of other's full self-expression. Her endless drive for everyone to have it all includes her awe-inspiring goal to create radiant financial freedom globally by 2050.

She is a Team Management and Leadership Program classroom leader at Landmark Worldwide. She leads Chicago, Illinois classrooms inside this ground-breaking technology. She has assisted hundreds of entrepreneurs over the last few years. She was one of the first certified One Thing instructors leading seminars, workshops and offering training with the innovated tools provided by the critically acclaimed processes created by Gary Keller, the founder of Keller Williams Realty. Inside her 30+ year real estate career, she has completed thousands of real estate transactions in every arena and wearing almost every single available hat. She has blazed unchartered trails and many economies over the last four decades, including the 2008 financial crisis.

At the age of 20, she was sponsored by Pretzel & Stouffer and became a paralegal in Chicago, Illinois at the field's conception, graduating in a paralegal pilot program at Roosevelt University that paved the way for paralegals.

Kimberly has been married to her rock and love of her life, Steve Genovese, since 1992. She lives in Valparaiso, Indiana. Their passion project is to establish a restoration center empowering people, animals, and nature to work together to create innovative holistic healing pathways for all.

Kimberly Genovese
Restpond Properties
4706 Cottage View Lane
Valparaiso, IN 46383
219-508-6742
Kimberly@RestpondProperties.com
www.RestpondProperties.com

Juliet Strocchia

Every Day Is a New Day

Today my life is very different. It's a life that I have chosen for myself. At a very young age, I made a decision that I would not live the life I knew as a young child. I knew I wanted to be a better person than my parents were. I wanted more for my life and was determined to define my life and not let circumstances define who I was or going to be.

My childhood was very painful. I often wonder how I even survived. People that know my past, can't believe I have not chosen a different path. My father was a drug dealer, and my mother was an addict. My childhood memories include sitting at the kitchen table, helping my mom and dad fold magazine pages into little triangle shapes small enough to put a dime bag of cocaine into. My father would then leave at night to go to random bars or clubs to sell the drugs. Sometimes he would come home and sometimes he would not return for days. When he did come back, it was with different girls that he would take into the basement. My mom was too coked up and passed out on the couch, to probably even notice what was going on.

I was only five years old, the same age as my daughter is now.

My dad was seventeen years older than my mom. He was previously married with two other children, when he met my mom. My mom got pregnant with me, when she was only seventeen. She even graduated from high school early to be with him. My grandparents did not particularly care for him, considering his baggage. However, my mom didn't care. She continued to date my father, regardless of what her family thought.

My grandmother was dying of breast cancer. She and my mom did not have the best relationship. I never got to know my grandmother, because she passed away just six months after I was born. However, I would like to imagine that my birth gave her joy and peace in her final days.

Even though I was very young when my grandmother passed away, I feel that I have a secure connection with her. I've heard stories of my grandmother taking me up to her bedroom and locking the door to play with me, while she was sick. When I think back, I have memories of her wake. It is very vivid and bright, even though I was only an infant. I would often mention this to my mom. The strange thing is, she claims I wasn't there. They thought it was best if I went to a babysitter. So, how do I visually see it if I wasn't there? I can describe it and feel it like it was yesterday. I have always felt her presence and as a child would speak to her and often pray to her. I still do today to both her and my grandpa.

My grandfather, aka Grandpa, was an amazing man!! He would give the shirt off his back to help anyone. I genuinely believe he's the reason why I am who I am today. When my grandmother passed, my grandpa was never the same. He was suddenly thrust into the role of a single dad to my seven-year-old aunt. I can't even imagine losing your mom at seven years old, nor can I fathom dying at forty-nine. That's how old my grandmother was when she passed away.

I am forty-four years old now. The thought of dying in five years is horrifying. My grandmother dying, is what I believe pushed my mom over the deep end, and when she became a drug addict. I think she has so much regret and guilt from their strained relationship, that her only perceived outlet was to turn to drugs and alcohol. I'm sure that my dad's abusiveness and infidelity also played a role. However, that terrible loss is what triggered her downward spiral.

Drugs were always available in my house, so I'm sure she felt it was an easy way to numb the pain. I remember drugs being on the kitchen table in little zip lock bags. My mom would tell me it was flour.

Random people would be in and out of our house all day. They would hang out in the basement all night and all day. Our neighbors eventually caught on to what was going on and hated us. The kids on the block were not allowed to play with my little brother or me. I will never forget one kid saying to me that they could not cross the line on the driveway to play with me. If they did, they would be in serious trouble. I can't blame them, now that I'm a mom. I would do the same to protect my child. That's our job as parents. I wish that my parents had made better decisions for my brother and me.

Each day was a new experience for me and my brother. It was one that no adult, let alone a child should witness. One day, I remember someone broke into our house, while we were home. They had a gun and wanted my dad to open the safe that we had in the closet. At first, my dad refused and acted like he didn't have a safe. My mom was screaming, and my little brother was crying. He was only three years old at the time and was scared to death! To be honest, I don't remember exactly what I was feeling. It was so surreal. I was only six years old and didn't really comprehend the scope of what was happening.

I can vividly remember the man picking up my brother with a gun in his hand, and putting a cigarette out on his head with his other hand. I will never get this vision out of my head for the rest of my life. My dad finally gave in and opened the safe giving him the money inside and who knows what else, possibly drugs. My mom then took a vase and threw it out of the kitchen window, hoping to get the attention of a neighbor or someone. The man then took everything out and ran out of the house. The police finally came, and we were all thankfully unharmed and safe.

To this day, no matter where I live, I will always have to have an activated alarm system with a ton of cameras.

During the summertime, my dad's mom would come over and watch my brother and me, while my mom was working. I guess you would call her my grandmother. However, I wasn't close to her. She was very mean, so I never really looked at her as my grandmother.

My mom was a waitress at a local restaurant that was close enough to walk to, in case she didn't have a car. My dad disappeared most of the time, so who knows where he was or even if he came home from the night before. The minute my mom left, my paternal grandmother would send my brother and me out of the house to play. She made us butter sandwiches that were disgusting! She then locked the doors and would not let us back in, until she was ready.

I remember many times being outside all day, pounding on the door because I had to go to the bathroom. I pleaded with her to let us back in. However, she would simply scream at us to go away and play. I eventually peed in my pants and had to remain in my soiled wet clothes, until my mom came home, sometimes many hours later.

I often wonder if that was the reason why my dad was the way he was? Was his mom this horrible to him growing up? I just hated it, when she would come over. She eventually passed away, and I hate to admit, but I was almost relieved that she wouldn't come over anymore.

I never knew who my dad's father was, and no one ever spoke of him. He was never married to my dad's mom. I don't even think my dad ever knew who he was. My dad had his mom's last name, which was the surname given to me when I was born. My dad eventually decided to change our last name legally, to what he thought was his dad's last name to start fresh, after supposed financial troubles.

I think he wanted a strong Italian name to go along with his lifestyle. He was always hanging around Italian men, some of whom my mom would say were bookies. Were they really bookies, or was that a fancy name for drug dealers? Looking back now, my dad was in deeper than anyone knew. His lifestyle led him to a life of crime and eventually jail.

Just when I thought that my life and the lives of everyone in our dysfunctional family were as bad as they could get, they actually got worse.

My dad proceeded to become more and more abusive to my mom. Their arguments over my dad being with other girls or having lipstick on his shirts or neck, escalated to a time of violence, where my dad threw glass plates, vases and other breakable things. One time, he picked up my mom by her neck and threw her down the basement stairs. Another time, he held a gun to her head and threatened her with her life.

My mom would hide with us in our bedroom, until he would eventually leave, or we would call my grandpa to come and get us. To this day, I still remember the Mickey Mouse phone I had in my bedroom, as one of the many gifts my dad gave me to make up for the horrible things he had done. I learned quickly that material things would never make up for the traumatic childhood I was living.

My mom started getting paranoid, which I now know was from drugs. She was doing it right in front of my brother and me. She was using cocaine and drinking a lot. He had an unlimited supply. My dad didn't care as long as she was off his back, so he could come and go as he pleased.

I would see white powder on her nose, and I would ask her why she had flour on her face. She would say, " I was baking." She was using drugs so much, that she claimed to see people in the bushes and would call the police. She even started to hang bells on the doorknobs, thinking that if someone were going to break in, we would be alerted. I still remember a big cowbell that she placed on the back door.

One day my mom was passed out on the couch in the morning, when I woke up. I got myself ready for school, even though I was probably only in the first or second grade. I walked to school that day. My dog got out and started following me. I didn't even end up going to school that day. Instead, I walked back home to bring my dog back. I opened the door and noticed water running. It was overflowing from upstairs. My brother, who was only four years old was trying to run a bath for himself. He couldn't turn off the water, and it was all over the floor. Luckily, he was okay and didn't get in the bath, because who knows what would have happened.

I saw that my mom was still passed out on the couch, so I tried to wake her but couldn't. My dad was still not home from the night before, so I called my grandpa. He came over and called the paramedics. They took my mom away because she had overdosed on cocaine. She was still alive. However, from what I overheard, she would have died, if I hadn't come back home that day and called for help. This would be one of the many times I would save her life.

Looking back, I often wondered what my life would been like if she had died? The sad part is that sometimes I even wished she had, so that I could have lived with my grandpa to get away from my horrible dad. I know that sounds awful to say about your mom, but I knew she was never going to leave him. I hated not feeling safe!

We would randomly move in with my grandpa, when things would get worse or when my dad would get arrested. However, we always had to go back. My dad would beat on my grandpa's door and even tried to kick it in, to get us to come back home. I also saw my dad being very abusive to my grandpa, both verbally and physically. This tore me apart. What kind of person hurts an older man, who cannot defend himself? I had lost all respect for my dad and absolutely despised him! I wanted nothing to do with him. I knew this at a very young age. I also resented the fact that my mom kept forgiving him and allowing him to hurt our family.

My dad was very manipulative. He was in so deep over his head with drug trafficking, that there was no going back. He was going to Miami, Florida every two weeks to bring back cocaine and marijuana to Chicago to distribute. It finally caught up to him, and he was arrested for the fourth time.

I will never forget that day. It was my little brother's birthday party, and the whole family was over to celebrate. The police raided our house, by breaking down our front door in front of everyone. How embarrassing, and at a kid's birthday party! They were afraid that my dad would run from the police.

Therefore, they waited for this day, in the hope that he would cooperate when his family was present. Our house had been under surveillance for quite some time. As it turns out, my dad was selling to undercover detectives. He never was the smartest man.

That night they took my dad into custody and seized drugs and guns from our house. My dad ended up taking a plea deal. They wanted him to set up the guys he was getting his drugs from. My dad agreed to do this, so that he didn't have to go to jail. They were offering him probation. The setup went as planned, and he ended up getting three guys convicted who spent seven to ten years in prison.

He was a lucky man to get away with this a fourth time. However, would he walk away from this lifestyle? It was all over the newspapers, my whole neighborhood knew and to top it off, even my teacher knew. There was no way out and nowhere to hide. Who would hire a convicted felon? It was all he knew. So, what did he do? He kept selling.

If you google his name, the headline of the newspaper reads "Man arrested for the 5th time on drug trafficking charges". Yes, the fifth time, and this finally put my dad away for seven years in jail. This was a blessing from God!

We lost everything, our house, our personal belongings, everything! My mom was devastated and crying, but I was relieved. We were finally free!

We moved into my grandpa's house and started at a new school. My little brother and I finally had a chance for a new life. Even though we didn't have separate bedrooms, (we had to share a bedroom with my mom and even sleep in the same bed), at least I could pretend to be a normal kid now, and we were safe. That's all I cared about. I thought to myself that maybe now I would have friends that will be allowed to play with me or even get invited to a sleepover. I couldn't wait to start fresh.

We were settled in, moving on with our lives and trying to act like an average family. Drama then struck again! We found out that my dad's sixteen-year-old niece was pregnant with my father's baby!! Just when I thought my dad couldn't get any more disgusting, he did! The summer before my father was arrested for the last time, his sister's daughter had spent the summer at our house. Well, I'm sure you can guess what happened.

My mom ended up taking his niece to get an abortion, since my dad was still in jail. I have no idea if my aunt ever found out what her brother did to her teenage daughter.

For many reasons, this is why I was so glad to get away from this horrible man that my mom kept forgiving. Even after this, my mom would still drag us to visit him in jail. I never understood why. I wanted to run away, while we had the chance!

At this point, I was in third grade. Everything I've shared so far happened during the first eight years of my life. There is so much more that has happened to me since then and to be honest, is still happening to me today. My dad ended up serving his time and was released from jail. He would randomly pick up my brother and I and take us out for ice cream. However, he eventually stopped coming around. Every day I would wonder if he would show up again, or if I would run into him someplace. Was he even still alive?

One day in 2001, when I was reading the newspaper, I saw my dad's obituary. I always skimmed the obituaries for some reason, I always knew, based on the lifestyle he chose, that one day his name would be there. The paper I read was a few days old, and I had missed his funeral service. I don't even know if I would have gone anyway. I wasn't even listed as one of my father's children. I ended up calling the funeral home, only to find out that he was murdered. The police report was calling it a home invasion, and my dad was stabbed to death.

When looking at my daughter every day, I wonder why. Why do parents put their kids in danger?! How can they choose drugs or alcohol over an innocent child? I remember more from my early childhood than anyone should ever have to experience in a lifetime! Sometimes I wish I didn't; maybe then I could be the person I really want to be. Instead, I am this overachieving, hide my affection, perfectionist, workaholic, who had learned how to disguise all of her childhood pain.

My early childhood has left scars, that will never be fully healed. When you see me from the outside, I appear as this perfect person who is a successful business owner, a wife and a super mom.

I have been blessed with a husband who is an amazing person that puts up with my twelve-hour absence from home every day. He understands why I need to do what I do. He supports me and loves me for who I am, flaws and all. We have a beautiful daughter, and I have a thriving business as a hairstylist, a career I have always loved.

My friends don't understand why I tend to keep myself so busy. They often get frustrated by my busy work schedule that does not allow me time to hang out with them. I tend to bury myself in work. That is how I deal with the constant struggle of my past. However, there is a bonus to this problem, which is that my business thrives, but my home life sometimes tends to suffer.

My early childhood was anything but pleasant. However, I knew deep down in my soul that I was going to be very different than my parents were. I wanted more for myself. I chose to live my life differently and create the life that I always wanted for myself.

To this day, I still struggle with some of the things that I feel have come from my childhood, such as always keeping busy. However, I recognize these traits and work on them every day.

Each day I appreciate the family I have and the positive people that I have brought into my life. One of the positive things that has come from my childhood situation, is that it has made me a stronger person and taught me that I am capable of doing whatever I put my mind to, no matter what situation I have experienced.

Some helpful tips that motivate me to continue staying positive are surrounding myself with positive, successful people and reading books. I listen to books on Audible. While I am driving is the best time for me, especially on the way to work.

A few of my favorites are:

- *The 5 Second Rule* by Mel Robbins

- *The 10X Rule* by Grant Cardone

- *Girl, Wash Your Face* by Rachel Hollis

- *Find Your Why* by Simon Sinek

- *The Go-Giver* by Bob Burg and John David Mann

All of these books taught me numerous life skills, so that I don't get off track. They have helped me to set goals for myself and to dream big!

Every morning, I read inspirational quotes to help me get started with my day. Every day is a new day, and some are easier than others. That's OK.

When I look back, I can't believe I have made it this far. Sometimes I don't even know how I got here, but I thank God every day for blessing me with this great life.

Juliet Strocchia

Juliet Strocchia is a stylist, licensed cosmetologist, and Co-Owner of The Mixx Hair Salon in Elk Grove Village, IL. Her passion is making women feel confident and beautiful. Before opening The Mixx Hair Salon, she owned her own beauty salon, JS Salon, also in Elk Grove Village, IL. Her successful career includes being a stylist for 17 years with advanced training from Mario Tricoci, Redkin, Paul Mitchell, Pureology, Matrix and the Redkin Exchange, becoming a Certified Colorist. She has styled hair for the Chicago Rush Dancers, Chicago Blackhawk Ice Girls and a professional comedian who has appeared on the Chelsea Lately show. Juliet enjoys spending time with her daughter Bella and husband Mike. She is an avid dog lover and has three fur babies of her own. Her family is most important to her, and she loves spending time and going on adventures with them. Juliet continues to advance her personal and professional growth through workshops and self-development.

She has always wanted to share her own story in the hope that her story will inspire and motivate you to overcome any challenges and obstacles that may come your way.

Juliet Strocchia
The Mixx Hair Salon
1090 Gloria Drive
Elk Grove Village, IL 60007
773-744-0143
JulietStrocchia@aol.com
www.TheMixxHairSalon.com

Amanda Tobinski

My Biggest Fear Becomes My Life's Work

"We gain strength, and courage, and confidence by each experience in which we really stop to look fear in the face… we must do that which we think we cannot."
—Eleanor Roosevelt

I love this quote by Eleanor Roosevelt. I think it truly embodies what it is to be fearless. I believe that the number one thing keeping people stuck where they are in life, is fear. This includes fear of the unknown, fear of what could go wrong, fear of rejection, fear of failure… I could go on. Fear is one of those things that keeps everyone paralyzed where they are, instead of blossoming into their full potential and to the incredible future that is waiting for them.

I want to discuss how fear may be keeping you stuck and provide some methods that you can use to, perhaps not overcome your fear, but be able to experience the feeling and the emotion of fear and take action despite it. It will allow you to take action to produce the life of your dreams. It's an honor to be able to share these tips with you, because I've walked with the challenge of fear throughout my life.

The journey of facing my fears began a long time ago. I was once completely terrified of technology, and that's putting it lightly. I was filled to the brim with a self-limiting belief that I was just not good with computers. I don't understand technology; it's just not my thing. My fear of technology was not unfounded. I was admittedly terrible at utilizing any type of technology or computers whatsoever.

In my college days, I suffered a humiliating experience the very first time I needed to use an online message board within my college curriculum. We had to use these online systems to communicate with each other, but it had to be done virtually. I remember being very scared and intimidated to go through this process and communicate with people through the online chat platform. I was very afraid, now coming face-to-face with all my limiting beliefs of not being good at this.

As luck would have it, it did turn out to be the worst-case scenario. I posted all of the content that I needed to, as far as completing my coursework for the online communication portion, except I had done it in all the wrong classes. I was discussing chemistry within an art class, posting about art with an English class and so on. I was utterly mortified when I needed to go back to class and face all of my fellow students in person. They were all going to know that I was the girl who did not have any idea what she was doing on the computer, and I was the ONLY one to make such an embarrassing mistake.

The fact that innovation through technology ultimately became my life's work is astounding. One of the many reasons for you to believe in yourself, is that regardless of what you are fearful of, that *very thing* might be exactly what you are put on this planet to do.

My belief system was not ultimately serving me at all. In the long run, it turned out that my biggest fear, my fear of technology, and all things computer-related, would end up becoming my life's passion, once I got over all of my concerns. But here's the thing, I'm not alone. In my collaboration with business owners and entrepreneurs, I speak with many people that are also very intimidated and confused by technology. It was not something that I was facing alone. There are many people out there that are just as confused and overwhelmed, when it comes to technology.

Later in this chapter, I want to share some steps that you can utilize in your own life to overcome your fears. It will allow you to move forward and truly create a life that you dream of, when you are not dealing with the crippling and overwhelming sense of fear. Many, many years ago, when I was absolutely terrified by technology, I could barely check my email. I was full of self-limiting beliefs that technology was not my thing. However, it became apparent that technology wasn't going to go away. I didn't have the luxury of being able to live under a rock and not make use of these resources that were going to be necessary, as I grew throughout my career. It was something that was inescapable.

I had no other choice but to face it. I was not going to live the rest of my life with these beliefs looming over my head, of how I could grow and further develop in my career. How am I going to be able to do all of these things, while also attempting to never use a computer? So, when I say that I was terrified of technology, it was a real thought in my mind of "how could I possibly find a career path that would allow me never to face a computer...ever." I was terrified of the idea that someday I would have to learn how to use a computer at all, let alone the various software. I had no idea about Excel spreadsheets or Word documents or even using my email correctly. It was a mess.

Once I had faced the fear, which was a very well-founded one because I was honestly so awful at technology and email, something inconceivable happened to me. Of all possible things, I was asked to help build a website. I felt, of all people, that I'm the last person that should've been asked for this sort of assistance. It was at this point, that I made the decision that I was no longer going to live in perpetual fear. From that moment forward, I was no longer going to let self-limiting beliefs control my life. I was going to face it, and I was going to figure it out.

I was very blessed to be raised in a family where I was told that you could do absolutely anything you put your mind to. If you place your heart and full effort into it, there is nothing you can't accomplish. I am so grateful for having that level of support from my family. I knew in the back of my head that if I just put my mind to this, I could certainly tackle it. There's nothing I couldn't figure out.

Since I was personally asked to help build this website, come hell or high water, I was going to make it happen. The universe had decided to bless me with this particular opportunity, and I was going to step up. So, I put myself to it. I decided, okay, I'm going to build this website. I'm going to go out and acquire all the resources that I possibly can, to figure out how to do this. I realized that if someone else has done it, surely, I can do it too.

I set out researching everything I possibly could to figure out the step-by-step process for setting up a website. I found a course that promised that by the end of the training, I'd be able to build a website. Amanda, the person that can barely figure out her email, was going to build a website. Thank goodness, the course that I took, totally delivered. It walked me through step-by-step exactly how to build a website.

At the end of it, I thought, "Oh my God, I did this!" I'm not going to be the person that's troubled by self-limiting beliefs that technology is the end of the universe. I'm going to be the person that knows how to do this. I built that first website, and I was so proud of myself at the end for facing my fears and getting out there, getting it done and tackling all the scary steps, one-by-one. When you're not comfortable with technology, every single step can feel like the end of the world. It all seems incredibly scary, every single click of the mouse. However, I trusted the process and screen by screen did the steps I needed to get this website out there.

Word soon spread from one person telling another that I had built the first website. I kept getting asked again and again, could I create another site? Could I make one for a friend and then for their colleague? This incredible snowball effect started happening. From the first website that I had no idea how I was going to cobble together, I then ended up producing over 500 more before eventually losing count.

At this point, I could let go of my self-limiting beliefs that I wasn't good at tech. As it turned out, many people around me weren't necessarily very good at it either. The only difference is that I was the one who was willing to face her fears and get outside of her comfort zone. This allowed me to figure out exactly how to go about learning this particular skill that other people were also pretty fearful of.

At the core, I'm a problem solver, and that's always been who I am. Now, as technology has evolved, the whole "if you build it, they will come" has become less and less effective. A website does not now necessarily equal traffic. The next evolution of my business was focusing more on traffic, and how to get people excited about your website and to know your brand. This is results-based marketing and branding. I work directly with business owners and entrepreneurs to craft marketing campaigns that will deliver the specific results that they want. I also work a lot in the field of automation, making sure that all the different platforms integrate. As the technology evolved, it required me and my business to also continually adapt. Let me tell you, all of those self-limiting beliefs kept creeping back up.

At the end of this chapter, I'll share with you some steps that you can take to quiet down those self-limiting beliefs and face your fears. While it may not eliminate your fears, it's going to allow you to recognize them for what they are and take action in spite of them. As the tech world evolves and changes rapidly, I still recognize these fears that come up again and again. However, I now have the tools in place, so that even though I can feel the emotion of fear, I see it for the false belief that it is and take action anyway.

There are still times that I stop and reminisce on how in the world did this girl who could barely check her email, now have an entire business focused on technology and automation? It's fascinating to think about it, looking back. There are an amazing number of apps and platforms that can streamline your business and life, as long as you know how to use them effectively. Since technology is something that is often a barrier to success for entrepreneurs and business owners, I've made it my mission to bring my passion and excitement to streamline their processes. I help them to leverage technology to their advantage, in order to ensure that they are getting the results they desire without having to suffer through all of those overwhelming tasks.

I mentioned that fear continues to come up for me, even though I've been in this business for over a decade now. Technology evolves very quickly. There are always new platforms coming out. Do I know what the next evolution of technology will be? Nope. However, you can bet that as business owners begin to encounter new problems, I'll continue to be their problem solver. As new things evolve, I will be on the forefront, learning and growing to be there with a solution.

Let's talk about those self-limiting beliefs. I mentioned the thoughts of fear do still creep up on me. It's not something that you get rid of entirely. I certainly cannot teach you how to be completely fearless, as a healthy sense of fear is part of being alive. As part of the human experience, it's not something that you're going to eradicate from your life completely. Fear is just a feeling in your body. It is no different from happiness, excitement, or sadness. However, I can definitely help you with some tips on how you can start recognizing and overcoming the limitations it brings.

The first tip is one that took me a while to fully grasp. It's that your feelings come 100% from your thoughts and your beliefs. Stay with me on this.

When I was terrified of technology, I was *choosing* to believe that I was terrible with computers. Yes, I certainly had proof to believe that I was bad with computers because I was always messing things up. However, I chose to seek out and remind myself of all those times that I was royally screwing things up. I was completely ignoring all the times that I had done things right. Our human minds have a way of focusing on the worst things as a means of keeping us safe. That was super helpful back when we were hunters and gatherers, just trying to stay alive every day. Today, this mindset is becoming more of a hindrance to our growth.

You see, our minds are designed to keep us safe, and the way they do that, is by making sure that we're not going out and doing things that we're unfamiliar with. When we are facing something that we haven't done before, and it's utterly foreign to us, the brain produces this emotion of fear in us so that we'll back up. We'll go back to that comfort zone and back to the comfort of our familiar places, where we know exactly how things are occurring around us.

Unfortunately, if we're staying safe and staying within our comfort zone, we're not experiencing any measurable growth. If you want to reach goals that are beyond where you are right now, you are going to have to get outside of your comfort zone. With the way that our brains are wired, trying to keep us safe, we're always going to have those feelings. However, we have to learn how to recognize and manage them, as a means of being able to move forward and achieve our grandest goals.

The second tip that I want to share, is to come to terms with the fact that failure is the fastest way to success. I'm sure some of you are thinking, "No. Okay, I'm getting off the bus. I don't want to believe that failure is the way to success."

Once you accept that some failure is absolutely necessary to achieve your goals, it's going to take a lot of the sting out of it. Much of the time, our thoughts and fears about the worst-case scenario are far worse than anything that could possibly happen. Our brain has a way of coming up with these outlandish ways that things are going to go wrong, which aren't even within the realm of possibility. We set ourselves up for total failure, because we allow our brains to take over and convince us not even to start.

I challenge you. If you just wrap your mind around the fact that failure is the fastest way to success and that some failure is inevitable, then it will be much easier to handle. You will anticipate that something may very well go wrong, but at the same time, you can still move forward. Expecting that you'll have a minor mishap to correct versus the whole thing blowing up, will open your mind to being okay with the fact that occasionally things are not going to go as planned. Even things going 50% in the direction you wanted, is way better than you not taking action at all.

You'll begin to welcome it because failure is showing you what you're going to do differently next time. Moving 50% or 75% toward your goal, while it's labeled a 25% failure, you're still 75% closer to the thing that you wanted, and that is tremendous! That's how you make exponential leaps towards your goals and toward building the life that you desire.

The third tip I want to share with you is that your future is not based on your past. I want you to sit with that for a minute. Nothing that is behind you, nothing that you have already done in life is dictating where you can and will go in the future. When we're talking about significant life changes or big goals that we have ahead of us, we often look for proof from our past. We look for examples of when we have done something that would lead us to believe that we can do this next big goal. Conversely, we also look for proof from our past, of ways that we've failed at this before.

This was absolutely true for me. When I was first diving into technology, I was so overwhelmed with my self-limiting beliefs about all the times that I had screwed things up with a computer or email or technology in general, that I was using it as proof that I could never succeed at it going forward. I was never going to be good at it. However, that thought was not serving me. I had to take all of the proof from my past that said I couldn't do it and acknowledge that the past had nothing to do with the future.

One of the examples I've heard many times, surrounding the need of proof from our past to verify that we can do something in the future, is that if it were true, none of us would be walking. As babies who are first learning to walk, we have no proof that we can. We simply keep trying again and again, then eventually we get up on two feet. We take one step. Yes, we're stumbling. Yes, we're falling, but over time, we develop the skill of walking. There was no past proof that we could and yet we did it anyway.

So, if you're feeling stuck on your big goal, if you feel like it seems too big and you don't have any proof that you can move forward and get it accomplished, remember that even as infants, we intuitively know how to move forward. Even if your brain is screaming that you absolutely can't see the path to get there, know that deep inside you have the skills and the ability to move forward, without proof of success in your past. That tip is really big.

The fourth tip that I want to give you, is to make a list of all of your accomplishments. I want you to have a really long list of all the things that you were not sure how you were going to accomplish when you got started, but somehow you figured it out, and you met with success. No accomplishment is too small! This should be a long list that's celebrating everything that you've done in your life that was a goal for you, such as graduating high school, graduating college, getting that raise at work, getting promoted… anything like that. These are times that you stuck with it, and you accomplished your goals.

I want you to make a list of all of those things. This is because whenever you're feeling down, or you feel like you're not sure you can get through a particular task or hit your goals, I want you to go back to your accomplishments list and realize that you've got this! You've truly accomplished amazing things that you didn't necessarily know that you could do. That list of accomplishments will certainly serve you well on the days that you do not feel like you can take action with your goals.

My final tip that I want to give you is, just for a moment, I want you to let go of any of your beliefs about whatever it is you are fearful of, and instead believe that everything about it is entirely neutral. What I mean when I say that everything is entirely neutral, is that there's nothing positive around your fear, and there's nothing negative around your fear.

For me, this was technology. I was terrified of technology, email, anything that had to do with a computer, and even my phone at times. I convinced myself that I was just not good with those things. There has been such joy in releasing those beliefs that were not serving me. Because we have control over our thoughts and beliefs, even for just a moment, I want you to believe it's completely neutral. The computer itself is not positive or negative.

It's only a computer, and it's completely neutral. Therefore, whatever your fear is, for just a moment, it's safe to let go of your beliefs and your thoughts about it and just let it be neutral. See it as the item it is, not through your lens of fear.

I go through this exercise all the time, because I recognize that my mind likes to believe and apply a positive or negative thought to everything around me. I make it my practice to continuously remind myself throughout the day that all things are neutral and that I can control how I want to look at it. This gave me the opportunity to either continue looking at technology as something that I was scared of, or rather, look at it as an opportunity to grow. I could finally realize the computer wasn't actually doing anything to me. The computer wasn't making me scared. That was me, scaring myself.

Once I realized that I could look at it from a whole new perspective, and from a completely fresh set of eyes that allowed me to see without the lens of fear, it became an opportunity for growth. There was nothing within the computer itself that was causing any harm to me. It was all my own internal thoughts that were causing my apprehension. Ultimately, those thoughts and beliefs were no longer serving me. When I discovered I couldn't move forward, while still believing I'm not good at this, I chose to believe differently. I decided to believe that it was an opportunity for growth and a chance to learn and grow beyond my current skill set to achieve my big, crazy goals.

I encourage you that when you're feeling fear, anxiety, or become overwhelmed by the thought of whatever it is that makes you uneasy; to simply take a second, step back and view it as neutral. Take a few moments to take a deep breath and acknowledge that there may be a different way of viewing this particular topic that's entirely new for you.

Had I continued to believe my self-limiting thoughts around how bad I was at technology, I wouldn't have this fantastic dream business that I have today… one based around technology build-outs, systems automation, analytics and all things tech. If I had continued down the path of listening to my own self-limiting beliefs that were saying I wasn't good at those things, I would have never arrived at the place that I am today.

I encourage you to take a look at your self-limiting beliefs. Even if you can't entirely separate from them right now because they feel so real for you, just take a moment, step back and acknowledge whether or not those thoughts are serving you. If it is a thought that no longer resonates with you anymore, if it's not an identity that you feel is going to serve you going forward, choose to believe something different. Ultimately, you can be and do anything that you desire. You just have to make the decision.

I want you to know that you have everything you need within yourself right now. You might not currently have the knowledge, or the skill set you need to hit all of your big goals. However, you do have the ability, capacity, and willpower to get anywhere that you want to go. You can do anything that you choose. It really is just that simple. Decide that you're going to do something, and then take massive action.

For more free tips on facing your fears, visit www.FreeFearlessResources.com.

Amanda Tobinski

Amanda has spent the last decade implementing growth strategies for business owners, entrepreneurs, speakers and coaches. Through her programs and private coaching, she teaches how to leverage the power of technology to grow your business without suffering from overwhelm. Through Amanda's work building automated systems to create customized client nurture and conversion campaigns, she has assisted many business owners in providing an amazing customer experience, while also freeing up time to focus on their strengths and ultimately providing more value out into the world. She empowers entrepreneurs with the necessary technology to scale and expand their message to reach more people. When it comes to her BIG WHY, providing value that positively impacts lives is the number one goal.

With her years of business experience, as well as being a Certified Life Coach, Amanda guides entrepreneurs to see beyond their current challenges to what is truly possible for their business. Having faced her own fears around technology, Amanda has a personal understanding of the issues that business owners face in the ever-expanding digital era. She firmly believes that you have everything you need within yourself. You have the capacity and willpower to get ANYWHERE you want to go. You have the ability to do anything you choose. It really is just that simple. Decide that you're going to do something and then take massive action.

For more information on Amanda's current programs and FREE resources to grow your business without all the overwhelm visit www.MagneticMediaGroup.com.

Amanda Tobinski
Magnetic Media Group
16350 Bruce B. Downs Blvd, Suite 47507
Tampa, FL 33646
614-582-0249
Amanda@MagneticMediaGroup.com
www.MagneticMediaGroup.com

Mary Szenasi

Soul Retrieval: The Courage to Fear Less

When I think about what it means to be fearless, I revisit myself in many stages of my life. I was waif of a girl who was never *at home* or felt safe where she lived, a wily teenager with explosive anger, a young mom suffering from self-loathing and a woman in the early stages of life, who kept intimate connections and people at arm's length. These are some of the parts of me that come to mind, when I think about the relationship I've had with fear. These are some of the parts of me that I want to share with you.

In the words that follow, I will be telling you the story of how I moved from being a victim to a survivor, to a woman thriving in life and on a mission to help others to do the same! I think that it is necessary for me to caution you of trauma triggers.

Although I was born and raised in Chicago; I can count on two hands the number of states that I lived in prior to the age of six. For reasons I cannot say I understand, there was a lot of moving around. I suppose this set the tone, if not the foundation, for my feelings of never being *home*.

I was in the company of my biological parents until the age of six, when my mother packed up a garbage bag filled with our belongings and we made our way across the country from Arizona to Illinois. My maternal grandmother lived in Chicago. This is where I would stay for the remainder of my childhood.

My mother struggled with schizophrenia and manic depression and still does. This was often scary and peppered in violence. When she packed up our things and sought out a trip to Chicago, away from my father, it was with the idea that my father had molested me. The truth was that she came very close to crossing the line from concerned mother looking for proof, to abusing me herself. It is said that only when we are ready to deal with things, that they will come up to the surface of our consciousness. The understanding of that fragile line almost crossed during her inspection of me, was one of those things that did not come up, until I was already on the path to healing, and ready to receive it.

Although there were several times in my life where I said what he was accused of were not true, I grew to understand that the adults around me believed what was being said about my father. I remember being in the office with a counselor who showed me rag dolls, asking me to point to where my father had touched me. Out of fear of my mother, the knowledge of what the adults around me had been discussing and the memory of my mother looking for the proof of the abuse, I knew what I was *supposed to say*. To this day, I don't remember what *I did say*. However, I remember what I felt. It was Fear.

My father was 30 years older than my mother. Because my mother had me when she was eighteen and I was a product of consensual incest between the two, I thought maybe I understood why everyone around me would believe the claims she made against him. However, it didn't change the fact that I was not abused by him. Sometime after she and I arrived in Chicago, she had a manic and violent episode. This caused my father to come to Chicago to take her back home to Arizona. It was at this time, that I was left in my grandmother's care.

Although I was only in first grade, with very little life experience, the next chapter of my life began with me having a very personal relationship with fear. This included fear of violence, fear of *not* being listened to, *fear of being listened to*, fear of my body, fear of my mother and fear of where I might be going next.

When I think about what it means to be fearless, I think about myself as a waif of a girl with no life experience, who had experienced a lifetime's worth of fear. I recognize how it conditioned me to be the person that I was to become.

The constant moving from place to place continued in the next four years of my life. The only thing that changed was who was living in the home, where I lived. It was always a combination of aunts and cousins, along with my grandmother. During these years, I experienced indignities that I did not recognize as abuse for many years. I often wore the same panties for weeks on end, and shoes without socks. There was even one time, when my big toes poked out of both shoes. There was often a sexual undercurrent to the things I witnessed or was made a part of. It made me very aware of my sexuality, before I was old enough to understand what it all meant.

I was constantly ridiculed at school. I was bullied for the way I dressed and the way I looked. I often went to school without a shower, wearing dirty clothing. When I was ten years old, I played hooky from school for over a week. This was because I was afraid of some of the older boys, who would ridicule me on the playground. My grandmother was eventually notified, and I was required to return to school. I did not identify who the boys were, for fear of what might happen to me if I did. It was shortly after this, that I came to know my maternal grandfather.

I don't know how long he was in my life. I can't say if it was one or three months. However, I can tell you that I remember every time that I was left alone with him. During the entire time that he was in my life, I was being sexually abused. I was not the only victim of his predatory behavior. There were other children during that time who were his prey, and like me, lost pieces of their soul to him.

It was one of those other children who spoke out. They brought attention to the atrocities that he committed. In my case, one day he just disappeared.

I was ten, when I developed a fear of being myself. It was a fear of saying "no", a fear of expressing emotions and a fear of being seen. The biggest fear I had was one that I had already carried around for a while. It was the fear of *not* being listened to *and the fear of being listened to*. Ever since the day my parents left me in the care of my grandmother, I was allowed to spend time with my father when he would visit. I was allowed to be alone and travel out of state with him.

Therefore, I was very young, when I became conditioned to believe that the adults around me would not protect me from others, who would trespass on my body or my will. The conditioning stemmed from knowing that my father did not abuse me but also knowing that there were people around me who *believed he did*. This left me in a state of cognitive dissonance, when it came to trust. It grew into a fear of trusting people, a fear of counting on people *and a fear of what I was*, because of the things I knew about sexuality.

I developed a huge love for reading and writing poetry. I now recognize that they were tools for coping with the things that felt ugly and uncontrollable in my life. I'd fall into the realities that I found in books (both fiction and non-fiction). These places temporarily helped me to forget about the realities in my life. Poetry helped me cope in a different way. Having an outlet to release my feelings, became a blessing for me. This is because there was no other place to release them. Reading and writing proved to be temporary refuges from the things that continued to wreak havoc on my body and my soul.

In sixth grade, my breasts were already a C cup. The negative attention they gained from everyone, created situations where I was defending the natural development of my body. This heightened the shame that I had already felt about it. Years of being incessantly picked on by my peers, turned to having to physically protect myself from violence. As a result, I became an angry and violent teenager who fought a lot. I fought anyone who trespassed against me. Later, I was happy to bully the bullies. I couldn't care less about the dangerous situations I placed myself in, while dealing with the anger that I felt. It was anger that was directed at the world, my family and myself.

There was a shift in my life when I was seventeen. I found out that I was pregnant with my first son. I realized that in the midst of anger, shame and guilt, there was love.

When I think about what it means to be fearless, I think about myself as an explosive and hurting teenager who had experienced a lifetime of fear, abuse, neglect and violence. I also think about how it conditioned me to be who I was yet to become.

My son, in all his perfection, changed my life. It began the moment that I first saw his face, I knew that there was indeed such a thing as unconditional love. *Love made sense to me then.*

At this time, there had only been two people in my life that I loved enough to trust. However, even that trust was not strong enough to reveal to them who I really was. My closest relative and very first friend, Mike, and my lifelong best friend, Diana made me feel safe, unjudged and loved. However, they didn't know me. The ugly that I felt, the bad that I felt, the tremendous amount of shame and guilt that were the foundation of every choice I had ever made was the real me. The two people who were closest to my heart before the birth of my son, didn't know *me*.

I was to learn in a short time that I didn't know me either.

I took big steps for myself, while imagining a better life for my son. I left Chicago and moved to a neighboring suburb to live with my aunt and uncle. I had known them my whole life and had been as close to them as I could be to any adult. While I loved them and loved spending time with them, they were Mike's parents. *He* created a haven of safeness for me. Mike would be close by and my son would be born into a home where he was loved *and safe*.

I learned some lessons about what a family is and what it means while living in their home. They laid the foundation for a steady relationship with two of the most amazing people in my life to this day. Although this move was an integral part of my journey with the people who I now call "my parents", I still had much to learn about what it means to live through life shrouded in fear. I did not stay in their home for very long after my son was born. Instead, I ventured back out to Chicago to keep learning the lessons necessary for the evolution of my soul.

For the next seven years, I ebbed and flowed out of dangerous situations, drunkenness and superficial relationships. Superficial felt safe. So did the numbing that came along with drinking. All along I tried to do what was best for my son, keeping him fed, clean, healthy and safe. I showered him with kisses, spent as much quality time with him as I could and made sure that he never needed or wanted for a thing! At least, this was how *I imagined it*. I wasn't yet at a place to realize that the way I was treating *myself*, directly affected and endangered my son. My anger never dissipated, and the excessive drinking never lessened. I spiraled out of control so much, that I was going to work still drunk, having only slept for a couple of hours the night before. The more I drank to numb my anger, the angrier I felt. I could not find my way out of the spiral. I turned the anger and the feeling of helplessness into a deep self-loathing. My feelings of guilt and shame heightened, while I drowned in the sea of my hangovers, regretting the things I had done (or not done) while drinking.

During my 20's, I had developed a passion for astrology. It was something I had stumbled on before the birth of my son and it stuck with me as a hobby. Over the years, I had accumulated so much information on the secrets of astrology and its connections to myth, folklore, symbols, alchemy, archetypes and psychology that I started casting birth charts for friends and colleagues. It was the beginning of a lifelong passion for seeking out the story of lost soul pieces, and the process of their retrieval. I made quite an impact on the people around me, by doing their charts. That is until I became unreliable, drunk or hungover and unable or unwilling to commit the time to my passion. During these years, I continued to use the coping tools that I had found as a preteen. Reading and writing were daily practices, no matter what state of numbing I was in.

I didn't realize it yet, but the continued escape that I found in reading was going to be the path to my own soul retrieval. Before this could happen,

I had to take another big step and another big move. At twenty-five, I met the father of my second son and moved out of Chicago to the neighboring suburb of Roselle. In the years preceding the birth of my second son, my whole inner life came crashing down upon me. I was no longer as explosively violent, but I was still explosively angry and trying to numb. While working as a medical assistant in Chicago and making the daily trek to work and back from Roselle, I gained over 40 pounds, started losing handfuls of hair, developed chronic headaches and struggled with a worsening feeling of unhappiness.

Unhappiness was the theme of my inner world. However, I seemed to hide it well with my happy demeanor. I was living with a happy persona that was not entirely me. It wasn't entirely fake either, but it definitely had its foundation in partying and drinking, rather than in being who I genuinely was. I knew I was more than who everyone saw me to be, and I was *way more* than who I had always thought I was. I just felt lost each time I'd try to tap into the deeper, less superficial me. I felt lost and scared.

There is great potential for change in our lives, when we realize that we are not who we have always known ourselves to be. When we become curious, even if the curiosity is shrouded in fear, anxiety and skepticism, there is an understanding that we are something *more*. This brings on hope, and hope is empowering!

When I think about what it means to be fearless, I think about myself as a young woman who was in a continuous storm of self-loathing. However, I had wanted to tap into who she really was, by collecting her missing soul pieces. I think about the woman who decided one day that she was going to ride that wave of hope and *fear less*.

From that day forward, I went through some of the most difficult challenges to date. *Change and breaking patterns*. I started working towards improving the condition of my physical, emotional and spiritual health. I implemented a diet and exercise regimen, which resulted in the loss of all my gained weight, the end of my chronic headaches and the end of my hair loss.

Meanwhile, I combated anger and the desire to numb with *self-compassion*. Shortly after the birth of my second son, came the close of my relationship with his father. I began a new chapter of life, as a single mom in her 30's.

The next few years of my life were heavily focused on healing a lifetime of spiritual wounding. It proved to be both a struggle and a great freedom. I stopped partying as frequently, which resulted in the clear-headedness needed to wrap around my self-development. My passion for reading, writing, astrology and the healing arts took up a large part of my time and were tools that I used to chip away at the walls of negativity, which I had built around myself.

While working on unpacking my childhood traumas and exploring what it meant to show myself compassion, I stumbled upon a corner of depth psychology that was unknown to me. It would grow to be the cornerstone of the healing that took place, while on the road to self-love. This tool was called *Shadow integration*. There was a seamless transition from being deep in my spiritual journey, to working on the psychological aspects of my healing. As it turned out, intentionally working within the realms of the psyche was comparable and ran parallel with all the work I had been doing spiritually.

I would often feel as though I had taken multiple steps back after only one step forward, but I would remind myself that fearing less would get me past the stretch. I learned that deep honesty and vulnerability were *mandatary*, while learning about myself. In addition, self-compassion was necessary, while working on soul retrieval through Shadow integration.

I actively worked on less fear of saying "no", less fear of the vulnerability needed to execute radical honesty and less fear of the unknown. This allowed the emergence of my true self to be nurtured. Every single day was a struggle. Every day I had to make a conscious decision to face my fears, by being compassionate toward them. At the same time, I had to put them on the backburner to make room for transformation. I found that one of my routine mantras was *"You don't have to be fearless; you just have to fear less."*

Looking back, I know that the biggest lesson that I had to learn was that taking responsibility for myself was necessary. I had to eradicate the conditioning of years of pain, fear and abuse and turn it into knowledge, self-compassion and motivation. I made a promise to myself that while on the journey of uncovering and collecting all of my missing soul pieces, I would do these things:

- Make a conscious decision to choose courage over fear, every day.

- Commit to the changes that need to be made, in order to break patterns that invite toxicity.

- Let go of people, habits and ideals that (re)create self-sabotaging environments.

- Be patient, compassionate and loving with myself.

- Keep learning and keep searching for tools to assist in the self-development needed to overcome the traumas left in the wake of my childhood abuse.

During this transformative time of my life, I realized that true fearlessness is merely finding courage in the face of fear. It doesn't mean that we *don't fear, or that we cannot feel afraid*. It is rather that we commit to tapping into the courage it takes to overcome it. *We must do what needs to be done despite it.* This was the marker of the beginning of my great transformation. This was when I began to see *who I really was* and what I was truly made of. I saw who I was underneath the blanket of shame and guilt. I saw who I was, without the need to blame others for my circumstances. I saw who I was, when I showed myself love, compassion and acceptance.

I'll tell you something, *I was truly amazing!*

As I started seeing signs of growth and these changes started creating new opportunities for me, the biggest and most life-altering thing happened. I met the man that would soon become my husband.

Prior to meeting him, I had learned a lot about the benefits of setting healthy boundaries, saying "no", giving and receiving from a place of vulnerability and what it means to love myself, above all else. Although I was still in the beginning stages of these very valuable discoveries, I was open to trusting and receiving the type of love which, for many years, I thought didn't exist.

Unconditional...

The very first time I met Claudiu, I knew he was the one! In light of honoring my healing, I shared with him childhood stories that I'd rarely shared with anyone. I was amazed to discover that he was on the very same path as myself and came from a very similar background. We immediately formed an intimacy that I had never known was possible. It was a companionship that was built around mutual trust, unconditional love, respect and vulnerability.

I remember a time when I would have pushed such a remarkable man away. I would have been suspicious of his intentions and motives. I also remember a time when I would have thought he was a *miracle*. I am proud to say that during the time I have grown to know and love my husband, the truth has become increasingly evident. He is able to love me so fiercely, because I love myself just as much. He is able to show me compassion, support and respect, because I have paved an easy path for him to follow. The same applies to my love for him. We are not miracles, but merely mirrors and a representation of a life dedicated to fearing less.

It was with his love, support and encouragement that I decided to enter the next chapter of my life. I started my holistic wellness practice, where I coach my clients to do what I have done. This is to stop living life as victims or survivors, while transforming them into thrivers. I guide my clients using compassion and experience, down the path to radical honesty, radical discovery and radical wholeness. I show them that on the other side of healing, is the full spectrum of the human experience, and it's amazing. There is nothing that we cannot overcome, when we make a decision to do it and we commit to that decision.

When I think about what it means to be fearless, I think about how being curious, making a commitment to change and a conscious choice to fear less, allowed me to overcome great odds and to bypass a life of mediocrity.

We all suffer from soul loss. We all suffer from things that drive us into survival mode, leaving us later in life to feel shame, guilt, sadness, anger, denial and confusion. We feel stuck. These things condition us to live life as only a fraction of who we were born into this world to be. No matter what events brought us to our current situations, fear is the backbone to what holds us in place. It is a place that is far from our ideal state of wellness and thriving.

Tell me, do you feel like you are missing parts of you? Are they beautiful parts, creative parts or joyful parts? Does fear triumph over liveliness, happiness, adventure and self-love? Are you stuck in a spiral of negative patterns?

If so, I am here to tell you that everything you need to transform from surviving to thriving, *is already in you*. These things are found on the other side of radical honesty and making the decision to change. You don't have to be fearless. You just need to start with a plan to fear less.

Follow me... I know the way.

Mary Szenasi

Mary Szenasi is a holistic wellness coach and Shadow integration coach from Roselle Illinois. After working in the allopathic medical field for several years, Mary changed course and went on her journey to become a certified aromatherapist, herbalist and wellness coach. She is currently an active member of the National Association for Holistic Aromatherapy and the International Alliance of Holistic Therapists. As the founder of The 6th House, a holistic wellness practice that focuses primarily on the emotional and spiritual realms of the human experience, Mary guides her clients past the ever-elusive "stuckness" that everyone seems to be feeling during our times. Her goal is to empower others with the mindset and tools needed to conquer areas of stagnancy, dis-ease, unhappiness, challenge and hardships in their lives; past, present, and future. The primary tools she uses to help clients break patterns and support transformations are astrological birth chart analysis and

Shadow integration. She understands this combination of inner alchemic work and self-analysis to be the path of personal soul retrieval. Always eager to add to her personal toolset, Mary is ready to be a student again, and start down the path to a degree in analytical psychology.

Mary Szenasi
The 6th House
P.O. Box 72493
Roselle, IL 60172
312-451-7810
MSzenasi@The6thHouse.com
www.The6thHouse.com

Kimmi Darovec

The Fool's Crossing: A Rambling Journey

My heart dances through minefields
Taunting the souls of the faint

I'm startled awake by snarling yips and grunts. My Jeep, Bertha, is rumbling! It takes a moment to remember where I am. Oh yeah…asleep in Wyoming under a peaceful, starry sky. At least I was. What's happening? I inch my eye upward along the door, peering through the glass, silent as a mouse. It's a good thing they don't know I'm here. Mice are coyotes' favorite snack! They frolic, playing beneath me for several minutes more, before racing off behind brambles. I'm a giddy witness to the mystical magic of nature.

It's 4:30am. My mind replays yesterday's antics: Visiting Devil's Tower, the sunset, and drinking with construction workers shipped in from around the country. The knick-knacks and porcelain teapots featuring families of raccoons juxtapose burly men chugging Budweiser. The spunky, aged bartendress invites me into her lair, regaling me with colorful local lore. I giggle and turn the engine. Let's get moving. The Big Horn Mountains, rodeo, and my final destination in this state, Yellowstone, awaits! Hobnobbing with bison, prairie dogs, and catching Old Faithful in her glory is more appealing than some scant sleep.

This has always come naturally to me: The rambling adventure! (I've been pegged a gypsy, and have the hair to prove it. It's a colorful, wild mane. Equal parts ringlets and fuzz. All I need is bells 'round my waist and castanets clicking between my fingers.) What hasn't been as simple, is my quest to be truly vulnerable. It's one thing to be bulletproof, guard up. It's another to

ABSORB bullets...to have them become part of our DNA, yet be unaffected. I want that superpower, to be with any communication, and not have it derail me from my purpose in life. I long to share my heart and not be "taken out" when I get hurt or things don't go my way.

Vulnerability is the pinnacle of fearlessness.

The opening poem scrawled on a cocktail napkin in 1998, was inspired by my love of freedom. Our universe is filled with unlimited freedom, and people feel the backlash when they try to "take it from me." I attack to protect and deflect. At least I used to. I've trained myself to not react and "taunt," but rather to inspire others to dance WITH me.

It's 2006, I docent at the Lincoln Park Zoo, make art, and tend bar. Looking around for what's next, I see I have two strong pathways: 1) Along with my Graphic Design degree, get a second Bachelor's in Zoology, or 2) Continue in the field of art, expanding my listening of humanity through a therapy Master's. While at the zoo, training guests and Girl Scouts on animal husbandry and operant conditioning, I discover I love teaching and connecting with people. (I could've SWORN I wanted to be alone in some remote hole, or above it all, perched in a tree, documenting the movements of wildebeest for 12 hours a day, with NO HUMAN INTERACTION.) This is how I end up at the Adler School of Professional Psychology. I enter a two-year intensive Master's degree program for Art Therapy/Clinical Counseling and go on the coyote-romp road-trip to celebrate graduate school acceptance. I travel three weeks/8,000 miles out west, alone with my thoughts.

I'll be sharing anecdotes from my life and bouncing around like a Tarantino film. The timeline may shift between decades, jobs and relationships, but it'll all come together. Since I'm a fan of folklore and the Tarot, I'm relaying my story via the **Major Arcana**. These are the 22 cards illustrating the Fool's Journey, also known as the Hero's Journey. While we are all the Fool, we also embody the noble Hero.

I begin my pilgrimage the unencumbered **Fool**, the Hero of my own evolving legend. As I dance freely toward the cliff's edge, people warn me of danger. When fear isn't part of your vocabulary, you scarcely listen to others sounding the alarm. You ignore your social barometer. You're not afraid to look stupid, regularly laugh at yourself and life, actually FEEL fear but act anyway, are committed rather than emotionally attached, and you buck the "norm."

Being vulnerable is nowhere on my radar. My mission at this time: Reconcile my blatant dichotomous nature. This rift is most evident in my art. I range from meticulously detailed, dark drawings to bright, vibrantly-colored, textural paintings. These completely contrary styles look like they've been crafted by two different people! (Which is often how I feel.) I gravitate toward the shadowy macabre, yet I'm rarely serious. I'm always laughing, cracking dumb, distasteful jokes and don't get why people have to be so damn upset all the time. I also love going out and creating large-scale art events (with 100+ guests), but I dislike entertaining at home. I'm an extremist who rampages through life, hair on fire! BUT I also enjoy sitting in a singular, isolated position, making art. On road trips, I fluctuate between sleeping in my Jeep and staying in expensive hotels. I'll spend $150 for a sushi and sake lunch (for myself), or buy a last-minute ticket to Budapest, and I also enjoy bargain-hunting, haggling, and bartering. It must be that gypsy in me.

If you want a good place to begin your own odyssey, I'd say don't be intimidated by variety or your Diversity of Self. Create it! Poke it in the eye! Let variety know you're here and unapologetically forging your bliss on Earth. If each day begins exactly the same way, this chapter is for you. I'm not saying routine and structure is bad. (I start every day with a cup of Morning Thunder tea.) I'm simply saying, "Shake it up!" Be the Fool.

> Absorbing frequencies through polarities
> Nearness beyond reach
> The far away, nigh
> A frolicking fold of certainty

Trading hands for disorder
To be discovered.

Structure in chaos
Strolling moonlit oceans of wonder
No shell unturned
Heaven bows to prescribed ritual
Bypassing ordinary doubt
Creating mystery
Of a mission achieved.

As the Fool, I first encounter the **Magician** and **High Priestess**. The Magician card has me fully invest my energy and resources in grad school. He represents the rational course of action. The Priestess beckons me toward alternate learning adventures. "I JUST signed away two years of my life!!! Where can I go, Priestess?!" I'm pulled in opposite directions, attempting to balance my Intellectual vs. Experiential paths. The more beholden I become to my studies, the more I want to run for the solace of a mountaintop meditation stream in Korea! Ohhhhhmmm.

When you've traveled extensively, there are many places your mind can escape BACK to. This sadly limits your ability to create newly and to envision that blank canvas before you. This is especially true when your physical body is sitting in a stark classroom with ugly florescent lights overhead, in a downtown Chicago high-rise.

I do well in my Art Therapy program and graduate, despite my best efforts not to. I long to assist others through creativity and anticipate getting paid exorbitantly for doing so! I quickly learn this ain't the case. For a time, my contribution to society is enough. After completing my internship at Cook County Juvenile Court and working in the private sector with children with autism and ADHD, I notice my heart isn't singing. I love the kids I counsel and make art with, but I'm blind to my personal passions and ability to expand. After two degrees and proving myself, basically to myself, it smacks me: What

I've invested $200,000 and two years of my life in, is NOT going to fulfill my cosmic craving to be the ultimate creator.

I want more.

I participate in and curate art exhibitions to channel my inner **Empress**. She's the Tarot card immediately following my two diametrically opposed teachers, the Magician, and the High Priestess. I am the source of abundant freedom. I am the Mother Artist. Creative flow radiates through me, and I'm on top of my game! Until her counterpart starts questioning my "responsibility." Blah. "Simple, Sir **Emperor**! I don't have any!" This is why I tend bar. There is minimal responsibility. I show up, sling drinks, entertain patrons, clean the place, collect vast sums of money for a few hours of work and head home. This doesn't take much creativity and provides little room to teach. The real drawback of this free-wheeling lifestyle is those days when NOTHING is happening. I'm standing around for eight hours, drooling and staring into the blinking neon glow of a Coors Light sign. I'm annoyed rather than grateful: "I should be home, making art, not wasting my time here."

Sound familiar? We're never where we currently are. We daydream about the future, lament over the past, or justify that our precious time could be better spent elsewhere. We rarely enjoy the present moment. (At this point, my dichotomies, or opposing forces within, are screaming at each other!)

A teller of truths, the **Hierophant** offers a valuable invitation, often in disguise. This person is my boss who unceremoniously cans me, because of her life's circumstances. I love this job, work loyally for six years, and am incredibly pissed off by this "injustice." During a weekend workshop called the Landmark Forum, I forgive this person who "done me wrong." I see that my boss was only doing what she thought was best for her business. And given my thankless attitude above, it kinda makes sense. I drop my upset, like it's crawling in bed bugs and move on. The anger and hurt are just gone. (More about Landmark in upcoming pages.) Since then, Mary Kay and I have ridden rollercoasters together, and drunk Aperol Spritzes with Michael Shannon at the very bar I got fired from!!! (Well, Mr. Shannon doesn't drink orange sparkly cocktails. We drink our drinks. He his.) The Hierophant forces us to discover the world we've been ignoring. I realize I've turned my back on my divine calling to empower and inspire the world through creativity...and that being entitled has it costs. Thanks, Mary Kay, for revealing this to me.

The **Lovers** card is next. Love asks me to make a CHOICE between my current life and the life I could have. I stop licking my wounds, stand tall and begin making my living solely through art. No more bars, unless I'm hosting events there. After decades on this planet, I wake up and choose my one true love. I also choose my boyfriend and our financial expansion as a team! Historically when it comes to money, my thoughts have been, "This is mine. That's yours. Let's ensure the two ne'er shall meet." Haha. It's a whole new dynamic, being fearless when commingling resources, spaces, and funds. Even when I've lived under the same roof with lovers in the past, I haven't been invested. That was my lack of vulnerability rearing its scarred and slimy face.

See how insidious fear is? Even for a bungee-jumping, white-water rafting, globe-trotter.

My dichotomy is beautifully illustrated by the **Chariot**. This card portrays a figure commandeering a regal cart, drawn by two sphinx. One black. One white. I attempt to converge my divergent styles of art, my darkness, and light. I interview artists at street fairs, do online research and vainly try to meld my media, based on extraneous feedback. This accomplishes nothing but me NOT trusting my own talents. I also grapple with straddling the line between freedom and love. My shadow side dominates as soon as the subject of love or money comes up. What has me diagnose "the beast within" and accept my shadow, is the energy of the **Strength** card. On one extreme, I experience doubt and fear. The other extreme houses entitlement and my "sly opportunist" persona. If I can get away with something, I will! And I KNOW I can.

Even though I see, know and accept all of this about myself, I'm unable to impact it driving my EVERY MOVE. (Despite that Master's degree in

Clinical Counseling, no less!) Thus, my journey turns inward. Until this point, external forces catalyzed my quest. The **Hermit** has me barrel head-long into the Underworld, a mysterious place of self-discovery. I develop scarabs as my protective talisman. My hand-crafted, upcycled jewelry is the conscious gift of my unconscious. (See photo attached.) These amulets alter my "vulnerability frequency," especially regarding money and love.

I'm at an event, where vendors are moping and complaining. "Where are all the people?! I haven't sold anything." I instead employ gratitude. This event is DRY. I can't even have a glass of wine!!! However, I keep generating gratitude. Believe me, it's hidden down deep, six feet under. "I'm grateful for this opportunity. People love my vision. People pay me for my creations." Just then, an absolute GODDESS materializes, breathing life into my soul! She gushes over my scarabs, my keen eye and who I am for the world. The proud owner of TWO of my latest pieces wears them religiously, continually promoting me. The goddess and I are collaborating on an art/dance event in 2020.

The energies surrounding us want us to win! The key is altering our frequency. When things look glum, be the focused light. Don't be dimmed and dulled by the wattage around you…even if you look like a crazy person…a Fool! The white hot light of passion and purpose burns too bright for many.

With my passion sparked, I spin the **Wheel of Fortune**. This card asks what I'm seeking. What weakness has sent me on this journey? Again MONEY, my Kryptonite, specifically how to make loads of it through art. Another question is how do I make love last? (Endure. Not "last" in priority. That's the kind of thinking that's kept me alone!) Acknowledging my two biggest pitfalls, allows me to begin building something new from scratch. Until we accept who we are right now, there's no way to transport ourselves into a future of our own design. The Wheel clarifies my purpose: I AM an artist who empowers and inspires the world!!! Art is my living.

The **Justice** card marks my distinct departure from the old world, where my styles must be reconciled. Ordinary operations have no home in my new world. This unfamiliar landscape requires new rules for living. The most prominent is, "Have fun playing and experimenting without being attached to the result." I thought I was already doing this, but in the Underworld, I gain whole new levels of mastery! In this way, I'm an artist who empowers and inspires BOTH worlds. The new world has me finally see, no matter the style, ALL my art is recognizably, uniquely mine. Paintings, drawings, jewelry? All mine.

The **Hanged Man** is a revolutionary, indifferent to social approval. He can also leave you looping 'round the hamster wheel of your internal dialogue if you fail to see how to interrupt it. The moment I declare my purpose, old-world, familiar doubts flood in: "I won't make it." "Is what I'm offering important or good enough?" If I stay here, I'm trapped. Suspended in motion. Sisyphus pushing that rock up the SAME. BORING. HILL. For all eternity. I recognize the gravity of my eternal internal dialogue and stop hanging out with artists who are suffering, loathe money or think they shouldn't be paid for doing what they love. ("If I start doing photography professionally, I'll end up hating it." So, of course, it makes MORE sense to work a dead-end job, where I work like a slave and get paid peanuts. This way of thinking is insane to me!!! This is literally a friend/lover of mine's argument. I still adore him and wish him well, but no longer spend time with him. He used to be MY WORLD.) I go on the hunt for this conversation. Sniff it out! It's pervasive in my closest circles. Artists or not, this is how we humans are wired: "I can't possibly be paid for doing what I love." #UniversalConversation

I upgrade my frequency again, surrounding myself with people who are wildly successful in my field! George Berlin. Mary Porterfield. Andrew Spear. My peers and friends are flown worldwide to create their vision, guest lecture at the most prestigious galleries and educational epicenters in Chicago, and have permanent installations at Hard Rock Cafes internationally. My circle has shifted. This energy is contagious! When what you're passionate about starts kicking your door in, begging you to play, you can thank the Hanged Man for turning you upside-down.

To overhaul my life, it's necessary to give up what I know, and allow contribution from others…which in my mind equals sacrificing my freedom. My refusal to budge is ridiculous since what I really want is love and a partner to join me in making dreams reality. The **Death** card has me look at how I avoid that which must be sacrificed. I avoid sacrificing my freedom, by pushing away those who love me. Thankfully, one suitor stands solid. Jerry is consistent and persistent. He emanates a space where I become unnaturally, uncharacteristically still. The dichotomies and wavering between worlds cease. While scarabs are my protective amulets, Jerry is my guide to the Underworld. He is my **Temperance** card in action. My light in the darkness. With him, I can be vulnerable and fearless at the same time. I wrote this poem about Kharon, Ferryman of the Underworld, in 2011, long before I met Jerry.

Amorphous suspension of swirling particles
Formulating nothing
At the impasse of lightness and dark
The ferryman ushers souls through uncharted seas
Beyond the world we know
In each heart lies the key to secret gardens untended
Undiscovered.

At the helm, Kharon seeks the source of human frailty
With no elucidation, strength of will prevails
Truth, peace triumphant
A steely blade with tufted shaft
In perfect harmony
The souls rise up with steady surge, steering toward
Sanctuary.

When I let go of what I THINK freedom is, I'm able to CREATE freedom, hand-in-hand with someone I love. Someone who believes I can do and be absolutely anything!

During an existential quest, we often encounter Death, Temperance, and the **Devil** simultaneously. This incestuous intertwining of the three happens in an instant. Alone, however, the Devil card is best expressed through C.G. Jung's quote, "One does not become enlightened by imagining figures of light, but by making the darkness conscious." So I ask, "Where have I been enslaved by my shadow? What am I addicted to and suppressing?" A more deeply veiled answer than "love and money," is BEING RIGHT and knowing what others are going to say before they speak.

This is not clairvoyance. It's arrogance.

The truth is I don't care what others have to say. I think I know better. I'll bury "my competition," which is usually people who love me. Nothing they offer sinks in. People are left feeling stepped on and unimportant. And PEOPLE are the ones who buy my art!!! (I should be nicer to those guys.) This shadowy arrogance betrays all I strive for. Just like rambling road trips…it comes far too easy for me.

The cockier we are, the harder the **Tower** falls. This card shatters beliefs and ways of operating. I need some of that. I'm bored and living the same day over and over, constantly repeating the same tired, arrogant patterns in romantic relationships. How can I destroy my nauseating cycles and deeply ingrained notions, that I can't even see, in the most sudden, savage way? Enter the Landmark Forum.

Even with adventure always on my horizon, I have a nagging sensation that this isn't it. This isn't the life I'm destined to lead. Heartache and feeling like "not enough," rules my existence, even though I have decades of evidence demonstrating I'm MORE THAN ENOUGH. For example, when I applied myself, I'd get straight A's and probably would've been valedictorian of my graduating class, if I weren't such a party animal. My art was superior to my classmates, and I got away with murder. I did half the work and still got the highest marks, which made me NO friends. Looking back, I can see why. I took this power for granted. It's the way the world was, and I deserved special treatment. Deserved to do whatever the hell I wanted, whenever the hell I wanted to do it. I never saw the impact of being this way, until the Forum. Big surprise, I wasn't acting like this only in art class. These are the epiphanies slapping us in the face as we sit in our Forum with 150 other people, peeling back our hidden layers of humanity. While battling my views of love, money, family and anything I ever made up about everyone, including myself, it feels like life is ending. This is actually the beginning of my profound connection to myself and the world. With my past complete, I can now show a side no one knew existed! The Tower causes an explosion, a breakthrough, the construction of a NEW self. I'm vulnerable, visible, ALIVE!

I'd never say one education is better than another. Landmark is simply the most effective method I've found for slicing through my indistinguishable bullshit. Nothing from international yoga tours, to graduate studies in Art Therapy, to driving/flying 8,000 solo miles has given me access to my "crap," and how brutally silly it is, like Landmark. The Forum is my key to fearlessness in trusting myself and being stopped by nothing.

With the **Star** directing my next scene, what was previously inaccessible is now viable and free for the taking. The "elixir of life," flows freely through regions of my internal terrain previously uncharted. I've hugged my outer limits. My old world view of freedom and vulnerability is demolished. I create and adopt new world practices, fearless in my communication. This subterranean exploration has made the unconscious conscious. Writing this short chapter to touch my readers, has made this Foolish/Heroic process my reality. My eternal gratitude to you, the person turning this page. YOU, not just Jerry, are my light in the darkness.

The **Moon** measures whether travelers are truly masters of both worlds, and knows I possess the map to traverse my inner landscape. This card determines who can cross and recross the treacherous threshold between worlds. I've proven I can reach my farthest recesses at any time, and have infinite access to myself and my imperfections. I now love me all the more for them!

I blink against the bright, beaming **Sun**. This card readjusts my focus back to the ordinary world. My inner world has shifted. The outer has not. When people still know me as arrogant or that entitled opportunist, it doesn't deter me. I've emerged victorious, armed with implements of understanding from the Underworld. Through being vulnerably fearless, I trust my ability to listen for what's not being said in the outer world, and my facility to win people over! I'm awake, welcoming all that's available to me. Light and free to create, from now til' my dying day.

> Straddling worlds
> Perpetually falling, standing
> The elixir of life ensures
> No thing reigns supreme
> Jesters juggling, smiling
> Ballooned purpose crystallized.

> Enduring stillness achieved
> Harmony of sensory, ethereal realms
> Emotion and thought intertwined
> Nothing dislodged
> Flawless fluidity of space
> My fingers crafting all creation.

Approaching the edge of my blinking city, the skyline welcomes me home. The **Judgement** card affirms I've passed all trials and am fit to share "the elixir of life," my immortal wisdom, with the world. With you. I am resurrected and revitalized. For once, there's nothing hidden below.

The **World** card celebrates my triumphant passage through the Underworld and back. I'm open, trusting and in love! I love myself, my art and my man. I'm finally home within myself, mastering communication, and coaching others to fulfill their dreams. I socialize with my dynamic network, while cherishing and choosing my Diversity of Self. I know in my bones that this is where my power resides. This is my reward for being fearless.

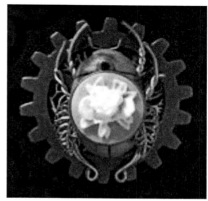

Kimmi Darovec

Kimberly A. Darovec: Artist by birth. Entrepreneur, coach, therapist, party animal, and human expansion catalyst by design.

1997—Bachelor's Degree: Graphic Design, University of Central Florida

2009—Master's Degree: Clinical Counseling/Art Therapy, Adler School of Professional Psychology, Chicago

As you'll read in her story, The Fool's Crossing: A Rambling Journey, Kimberly lives for art and travel. She grants credit for this passion to her Czech grandparents, who brought her on a National Lampoon's European Vacation at age sixteen. A knowing nod also tips toward the amazingly cool parents, who allow her the freedom to be and act. At sixteen, and eternally.

Born in Florida, this intrepid traveler put down roots in Orlando for nearly a decade. As a free-spirited crafter of macabre, overtly sensual drawings and vibrantly colored paintings, Kimberly has been spotted, naked, covered in paint, pressed against canvases, joyfully creating with her diverse community of fellow artists. Orlando in the 1990's was filled with weird and wonderful magic. Bonfires lit the horizon, and artists of all ages, from 17 to 75, danced 'round them celebrating life!

In the corporate world, Kimberly worked as designer/Photoshop Guru for Orange County Government, the Golf Channel, the Photography/Publicity Department of Universal Studios and moved on to be a trade show marketing Senior Designer, before moving out of state.

Kimberly spent eight months in the hills of Tuscumbia, Alabama, the birthplace of Helen Keller. (The small town's claim to fame.) There she connected with family, until 2002, when at 27-years-old, a local band of Rockabilly Hairstylists inspired her move to Chicago.

She never left.

In Chicago, Kimberly has won "Best in Show" and "Curator's Choice" accolades. She prides herself on her diversity of work and ability to adapt to any request or commission, yet maintains her unique, congruently incongruent style of art-making.

Kimmi Darovec
ChicagoARTery; Scarab Sanctuary
3563 W. Armitage Ave #2
Chicago, IL 60647
773-354-0391
Kimmi.ChicagoARTery@gmail.com
www.KimberlyDarovec.com

Heather Rosson

Purpose First

I have always been good under pressure. When I was ten years old, my parents bought us ATC three-wheelers. Remember those? One night, we decided to just do a quick ride in an empty lot across the street. My cousin, who was three at the time, was riding with my dad on his ATC, sitting on the seat in front of him. There was a dirt pile for a construction site that we had ridden on many times. However, that night was different. We had no idea that the construction company had cleared away a part of the pile, which created about a three-foot drop-off. My dad didn't see it. It was dark, and they rolled, head first, over the embankment. I was riding behind them. All I noticed was that the headlight from his bike simply disappeared. At least it was enough to make me stop. I jumped off my ATC and ran over there. It was only a three-foot drop, so it was easy to just jump down. I saw my dad with blood all over his face. He was conscious but not coherent. He was attempting to crawl out from under his ATC but not really able to. My mom and aunt had been standing in the field watching us ride. They didn't know that there was a problem, until they heard me scream. As they were on their way over, I jumped on my bike, rode home and called for an ambulance. This was before 911 was available in Phoenix, AZ. Luckily, my mom had the foresight to have emergency numbers taped to the side of the phone. My dad almost died that night and spent a full week in the ICU with extensive head trauma. My three-year-old cousin had three scratches on his stomach. My dad had wrapped himself around my cousin and protected him, with his head.

Every time I attempted to begin My Story for this book, I found myself stopping and then sitting down another day with a new place to start. I'm pretty sure the ideal place to begin is not an anecdote from when I was ten. So, I began to wonder why. Why is this story, my life story, so difficult to begin? It seems that other stories almost write themselves. We are all so used to the typical Hollywood stories. Did you know that most of them follow a very specific formula? In literature, it is called The Hero's Journey. The main character is usually casually moving through their life, when something extraordinary happens. The event is often a tragic one, like in my narrative above. The tragedy sends them on a journey or a quest. There is then some conflict. The hero overcomes the conflict, the princess is saved, transformation happens and they all live happily ever after. This formula creates a compelling tale that we know well and can be easily drawn into.

So why, then, is my own life story so difficult to begin? It is because real life doesn't order itself in this very linear Hero's Journey formula. There is no one beginning. We begin over and over again throughout life. Our lives are a tapestry of stories all weaving themselves together to create a beautiful image. The best part is that each new story we live in, is preceded by every story we have already lived. This is one of the reasons that I am adamant that it is never too late to begin again! There is a famous Chinese proverb that says, "The best time to plant a tree was 20 years ago. The second-best time is now." It is never too late to begin something new.

Nothing is wasted in God's economy. "See, the former things have taken place, and new things I declare; before they spring into being I announce them to you." (Isaiah 42:9) Did you just hear that? God speaks to you. He announces the new. We don't always notice him announce it though. I often hear people say that they don't know what God is saying to them. They are waiting for the clouds to part and an audible voice from heaven to tell them what to do next. Perhaps they want to know all of the steps, before they even begin. He is announcing each new thing to you, while building on the former ones that have taken place. Did you also notice that He tells you about it, before those new things spring into being? He needs us to take action on the purpose that

He has placed within us, in order for those new things to become reality. In Ecclesiastes, we read, "Farmers who wait for the perfect weather never plant. If they watch every cloud, they never harvest. Just as you cannot understand the path of the wind or the mystery of a tiny baby growing in its mother's womb, so you cannot understand the activity of God, who does all things. Plant your seed in the morning and keep busy all afternoon, for you don't know if profit will come from one activity or another - or maybe both." (Ecclesiastes 11: 4-6) Everyone has a God-given purpose on this earth, but how do we know what it is? When do we fulfill our purpose? Sometimes we need help hearing God. Help comes in the form of community, prayer and knowing the many ways God speaks to us.

After my dad had wrecked on his ATC, people kept telling me how fearless I was, that I just knew what needed to be done and put into motion the actions necessary to get my dad help, even before my aunt and my mother arrived at my dad's side. The problem was, I wasn't fearless. I was full of fear! I just acted, in spite of my fear. I honestly don't believe that fearlessness exists in the human condition. We all experience fear: fear of failure, fear of success, fear of dying, fear of living, fear of not knowing who we are and why we're here, fear of finding out who we really are. There is no such thing as fearless! There is bravery; there is courage; there is valor; there is confidence. However, there is no fearlessness. Therefore, what does it mean to live a life in a fearless way? It is not the Hero's Journey that looks at life through one lens but it is a way of living that looks at life from different angles. It is a way of looking at life through a holistic lens, where all of our stories are intertwined.

When I turned 35 and my youngest was starting all-day kindergarten, I knew it was a time of interweaving and transition. I had been fully immersed in motherhood for ten years and now my days were mine. For a while it was fantastic. I had all kinds of time to myself. I had time to go to coffee with friends, go shopping and be in my house alone. If you have had small children, you know the amazing feeling of a quiet house! It felt like complete freedom. I'll admit, there was a part of me that was like, "Woo-hoo, all of this free-

time is the reward for spending day-in and day-out with my small children!"
Then I started feeling a little lost. It didn't feel like enough. I hadn't done
enough. I hadn't accomplished enough. Everyone had been saying that starting
in your 30's, you begin to know who you are and why you are here on this
earth. However, I didn't. Sure, I knew I was a great mom and that one of my
purposes was to raise amazing children, who will contribute to society and
be kind, loving, successful human beings. I never doubted my desire to stay
home and raise my children. It's still a decision that if I had to do over, I would
make again. However, that doesn't mean that I felt completely fulfilled and my
mission was done. I knew there had to be more.

As I began searching for "more", I decided to go back to school. See,
that is my comfort zone, to just keep learning. When I was doing my undergrad
work, years before, I pursued two degrees: math because it's practical and I
can support myself with it, and religious studies because I liked it. I didn't
think the study of religion would be something I could create a job around,
especially one that isn't vocational ministry. At this juncture in my life, I
wasn't as worried about a job, so I decided to get a master's degree in theology.
School is something that I know I'm good at. I didn't realize at the time that
I was simply retreating to my comfort zone in the midst of feeling lost. When
I look at the decision to study theology in hindsight, introspectively, I realize
that my choice was one that rebelled against the idea of always being practical.
It was just something that I wanted to do. I didn't know it at the time, but
always doing things that are practical was one of the things that was killing
my dreams. The comfortable option is something that we all tend to gravitate
toward. Luckily, sometimes, if we let it, our action will propel us toward the
uncomfortable and allow us to grow.

Such a thing happened, while I was in my master's program. They
offered a class called Life Focus, in which we created a mission statement for
our lives. My mission statement, which I still refer to today, was "My purpose
is to help people create a space of rest in their lives, so that they can hear God's
voice clearly and live a balanced, full, abundant life." Before looking through

this lens, I had been content to think of my master's as just an opportunity for me to learn. Suddenly, I began to think of it as a way to serve. At the time, my goal was to open a retreat center for burned-out pastors and executives. That goal is one that is unrealized. However, just because I haven't opened a retreat center, doesn't mean that I'm not living in my purpose. Our purpose can take many different avenues of fulfillment. My purpose has been present in every decision I have made, because it is innate to who I am. I have created a space of rest in each endeavor as I have moved forward: teaching high school, my local service business and through the Blessed Business Builders Community and Purpose First.

I am intentional about listening to God through introspection and revelation, which is simply those ah-ha moments that we all have. However, not only does God speak to us as we reflect on our purpose, but He also speaks to us through major transitions and change. For instance, in the midst of managing the demands of school, a catastrophic recession affected our whole country. My husband had been a custom home builder. The housing and construction industries were hit especially hard and we decided to close that business. Luckily, we didn't have debt. We were one of the fortunate ones who didn't lose our home. We were able to tread water, until he got a job. He was working for someone else for the first time ever and we were making a fraction of the money we had been making. I know this is a common story for the time period. I also know we were very fortunate. However, it wasn't exactly the best time to start my own business. Looking back, I know that God was speaking to me in these circumstances; knowing that I would need to do what was best for the most important people He has put in my life, my family.

As we all often do, I retreated to a place of safety. For me, this meant the classroom. I knew I could quickly get a job. I was excited to create a space of rest for my high school math students, which allowed them to explore who they really are. What I didn't know is that 15 years after leaving the classroom the first time, it had become a very different place. My class sizes were huge and I couldn't do the job I wanted to do. It was impossible for me to be a great teacher in those conditions. I loved my students and I loved the impact I was making. However, the system was simply too difficult to work in. My comfort zone had become extremely uncomfortable. After only a handful of years, I needed out of the classroom.

We often leave situations like this feeling like we have made a mistake. I know that it wasn't a mistake to go back into the classroom. In fact, I often say there are no mistakes. There is only success and learning. I experienced both of those during my time teaching. One of the things I learned, is that God speaks to us through our experiences. Those things that feel like mistakes, God will use them. God doesn't *cause* us to go through the situations that we often put ourselves in. However, He will *teach* us through them. Our experiences become a part of our purpose. "And we know that all things work together for good to those who love God, to those who are called according to His purpose." (Romans 8:28) The trick is to keep moving forward and to keep looking and listening to His voice.

I think that sometimes people see my actions as fearless, because I embrace change. In fact, one evening a group of friends and I were having dinner together and I was telling them that I was going to leave the classroom. My friend Katie said, "That's what I love about you. When something isn't working for you, you just change it!" Until that moment, I didn't realize how much change and new beginnings were a part of who I am and who I was created to be. I am not talking about change for change's sake or change in a hasty manner. The year I left teaching, I knew in October that I was done. That doesn't mean I just quit in October. I finished the year. I prayerfully considered my decision. Through prayer, I realized that teaching was a comfort zone that I had reverted to, when times got tough. Was it really fearless to leave the classroom, no! However, it did take courage to put one foot in front of the other and actually do it. It took courage to embrace the change.

I remembered my training years earlier and intentionally created a business that allowed me to have a great business *and* a great life. I realized that it all starts with finding your Purpose First. Included in my Purpose First program is training called "8 Ways God Speaks To You Without Parting the Clouds." The most obvious way He speaks to all of humanity, is through scripture. God speaks to the collective humanity this way. We know that He cares about us collectively—He loves humanity. He loves His creation. However, He also loves and cares about us as individuals. "You are uniquely and wonderfully made" (Psalm 139:14) and He knows every hair on your head (Luke 12:7). Doesn't it stand to reason that He also has a unique, individual purpose for you and that you have a unique job to do here on earth? God uses the unique way He made you in the way that He speaks to you. Your life experiences are part of the clues you need to define God's purpose for you. Life experiences can be small (a child entering kindergarten) or huge (a nationwide recession). You have seen a few other ways interwoven in my story, for instance, in the way God spoke to me through my friend Katie. God often uses other people to speak to us. Our friends and family see things in us that we can't see in ourselves. We are simply too close to it. It will take courage to ask what others see in you!

We never reach a plateau where we get to stop listening! In an ironically compelling example, I was able to use my Purpose First model to examine my own business endeavor and fine-tune it to meet my needs. My local service business, AZ Moving Boxes, rents reusable moving boxes to both residential and commercial clients. There are a lot of things about my box company that I love. I create a space for rest during one of the most stressful times in a person's life—moving. I love that people are always happy, when we pick up the boxes, because it was so much easier than any other time they have moved. I didn't realize people could get so excited about moving boxes—but they do have wheels! I thought I had the perfect business. However, there was one thing that I didn't think about or realize—the business didn't fit my lifestyle. Through introspective engagement with Purpose First, I learned that I have a core value of flexibility and freedom. My box business created an environment where I served my mission but didn't fully encompass all of my needs. Needs can be something as mundane as escaping in the summer! In case you don't know, our temperatures in the summer can get up to 115 degrees. Respecting core values…I brought in a partner that now works in the day to day management of the box company.

One of the best results of knowing what my mission statement is for my life, is the ability to know what opportunities to say no to and what opportunities to say yes to immediately. The real question simply needs to be, "Does this opportunity align with my mission?" However, sometimes what exactly that mission looks like may change.

Our purpose in life is the meaning of our existence. We often go through life without the courage to be introspective and vulnerable, creating the illusion that our lives are insignificant. You and I have an enormous impact on the world around us. We have a connection with others and with a creation that matters. Your God-given purpose and mine have been with us since birth. "But the plans of the Lord stand firm forever, the purposes of his heart through all generations." (Psalms 33:11) God has given us all of the clues we need to figure out what that purpose is. Our vision may change and we may decide to do things a little differently. However, our mission and our purpose will never change. We simply need to discover it!

Heather Rosson

Heather Rosson is a business and financial coach, who helps Christian entrepreneurs create great businesses and full lives. She believes that a full and abundant life is one that has God and family at the center, work that focuses on others and leaves room for ministry, fun and rest, eliminating burnout. Heather strives for each client to create the life they've always dreamed of, by focusing on their purpose first. Heather owns a local service business, AZ Moving Boxes, and understands what it means to be in the trenches. Growing up in an entrepreneurial household in the construction industry, she knows the sacrifices that are often made, and the stress involved. Her upbringing and experience fuel her desire to see others find joy in their businesses. Heather's first love is teaching. She taught teenagers how to do math, love themselves, be kind to others around them and feel confident in what they are capable of. She always made sure that her students knew they mattered as people. She taught them the meaning of hard work, that perfection is a myth and they each have their own unique gifts and talents. When Heather left the classroom, she carried the same love of teaching into the world of entrepreneurship. Heather has a B.S. in Mathematics and a B.A. in Religious Studies. In 2012, she completed a M.A. in Practical Theology and a Certified Leadership Coach program. To add to her expertise, she became a Certified Master Financial Coach in 2019. Heather loves her Arizona desert life, with her husband and three children. Her greatest passion is to help others hear the voice of God in the way that He made them, through their gifts and experiences. She fulfills her purpose through coaching, teaching and speaking engagements.

Heather Rosson
Blessed Business Builders
4925 W. Gates Pass Road
Tucson, AZ 85745
520-609-5061
Heather@HeatherRosson.com
www.HeatherRosson.com

Jean Kadkhodaian

Reaching New Heights, One Step at a Time

I wanted to be an average mom with a normal job and accomplish an amazing goal. I was not someone that could hike the John Muir Trail, when I set that goal. Through discipline, dedication and perseverance I became a person who not only could but did.

It's not that I was depressed, as a teenager, but when I thought about being dead, it seemed comforting. Little did I know that years later, I would find my way to walk away from toxic relationships and self-doubt and into a life better than I ever imagined.

At 17, my family life was chaotic and overwhelming. There were daily conflicts between someone in my home of six brothers and two sisters. I worked 60 hours a week while in high school to avoid being home. My boyfriend at the time was concerned and took me to my high school counselor, who called in my parents. My dad simply said, "Snap out of it"."

I moved out that night.

That move was the start of many in my young life. I moved in with my boyfriend, only to be subject to his cheating. However, my world fell apart, when he announced he was going to college. I didn't think I was smart enough to go to college, so I joined the Army Reserves. He broke up with me. The pain was so crushing, it was hard to breathe for the first few days.

At the age of 18, I walked into a recruiter's office at 5 ft. 2 inches, and 144 lbs. (It is sad that I know my exact weight at all the significant points in my life.) The maximum weight was 127 lbs. I didn't eat, gave blood, took laxatives, and Ipecac to make myself throw up. I reached 126 lbs. in three weeks. This extreme weight loss plan destroyed my metabolism for the rest of my life.

On August 22, 1985, I was on a plane to Ft. Dix, New Jersey. I decided that I would reinvent myself. I would be bold and confident, no longer the shy girl hiding among my 8 siblings. For the first time in my life I was not someone's daughter, sister, or girlfriend. I was Private Zender.

I learned to discipline myself and do unusual things, like shoot an M16 rifle, launch hand grenades and marched 21 miles with a 45 lb. pack. This cute little blonde girl from the Chicago suburbs did not look like a typical soldier. However, the Army fit me like a glove. For the first time in my life, I had self-esteem, good friends and confidence. I was fearless and happy.

I settled into part-civilian, part-military life. Even though I was secure and confident in myself, I was no better at relationships. Dating was confusing. I couldn't tell the difference between being used and being loved.

Shortly after my 21st birthday, I became a mother. I was uneducated, had no money and was on my own. Having my son was a huge blessing in disguise. I had to get my shit together. I joined a support group and learned about myself. I decided I wanted to become a therapist. I also learned as an adult that I was dyslexic. This was the early 90s, and an invention called a word processor made it possible for me to go to college.

At 23, I found myself in a relationship with a guy in my Army unit. He was always unavailable. I could only wait until he called or showed up at the bar, where I bartended. I met his parents and his son and eventually his wife, although he still denies he was married. I thought to myself, "I could break up or I could stay with him and figure out why I keep attracting guys like this." I stayed with him for five years.

I was in the Army, bartending, and in a toxic relationship. I needed to make some drastic changes, so I quit the Army, quit bartending and moved to a college town. My son was five. I thought it would be easy to find a job, but it wasn't. A decent waitress job 45 miles away came up. I took the job, even though I had no heat in my car. I bundled up and even wore battery operated socks. The cold wasn't the worst part. Without a defroster, I could barely see driving home in the snow at 1:30 am.

My boyfriend never broke up with me. He just left me alone for long periods of time. I couldn't judge if a guy was a good person or not, so I stopped dating. I was happier when I was not in a relationship and decided to be single for the rest of my life. If a guy showed interest I'd say, "You should be glad I am not attracted to you, it probably means you're not an asshole." This upset my dad, but I told him, "It would take a hell of a great guy for me to change my mind."

By the time I was 30 years old, my son was nine, I bought my own home, after moving 8 times, and I loved working as a case manager. I finally felt like I was doing something right and started my master's degree. I was rocking it as a single person. For the first time in my life, I was happy most of the time.

Then I met Ray. We worked together and became friends. A few months later, he leaned over and kissed me. He also had been in a seven-year toxic relationship. Since we had both worked on ourselves, our relationship was amazing. Early on, we were both brutally honest about our wants, needs and non-negotiables. We were able to achieve the synergy that we had always longed for in a relationship. Each of us would have walked away, rather than compromise our core selves, as we had in the past. We were married on February 14th, 1998!

In 2015, three things happened: I turned 49, I watched "Wild", and I bought a Fitbit.

"Wild" is the story of one woman's 1100-mile trek along the Pacific Crest Trail. My new Fitbit showed I was only getting 1800 steps during a normal workday. I weighed 185, which is what I weighed six months after I starved myself to join the Army. I have lost and gained the same 40 lbs. many times since then.

I decided to hike 1000 miles and sleep 40 nights in a tent between February 20th and November 20th, 2016, my 50th birthday. My ultimate hike would be the John Muir Trail or JMT, in California, 200 miles over 12 mountain passes. My husband wasn't happy about me hiking alone and knew he couldn't talk me out of it, so he joined me. Our first hike was one mile and it hurt. A month later, we hiked five miles with 15 lb. packs.

By September 2, we had hiked 500 miles and spent 14 nights in a tent. We hiked in the Philippines, Japan, and 14 USA states. We hiked together, sometimes I hiked alone, and sometimes our kids, siblings, or friends joined us.

We didn't know what a mountain pass was, but on Day Two of the JMT hike, we made it over our first pass. The views were amazing, everywhere you turned looked like a masterpiece. On Day 10, at mile 93, in the dark, I tripped over a log. My ankle was swollen, and my toe burned.

The next morning I was able to put weight on it and support my 45 lb pack. We decided to keep hiking. I was slower and stopped often to soak my foot in the cold mountain creeks. Instead of the 10 miles per day we had scheduled to hike, I had to stop after six and a half.

We were in the middle of the mountains with no easy way out. I was exhausted physically and mentally. Stopping meant we wouldn't complete the full hike in the allotted time. We decided to press on. I was happy but in a lot of pain.

The next day the swelling was worse. I didn't want to take pain pills, because I didn't want to be uncoordinated. After the first painful mile, endorphins kicked in and I pushed on. On day 19 we sadly decided to stop 20 miles short of our goal. We completed 180 miles, 87 of which I accomplished with a broken toe and a chipped bone in my ankle.

Despite learning I had broken my toe, I was still determined to reach my goal of 1000 miles. I had to hike six miles, every day, for the last 62 days until my birthday. On November 20th, we walked down French street to Café

Negril. The last step of 1000 miles! We celebrated my 50th birthday with some bourbon, dancing the night away to the beautiful music in New Orleans. Every step had been worth it.

A person in pain has two choices. They can seek comfort or choose discipline. Most of us seek comfort from pizza, wine, and ice cream, which is temporary. The behaviors that bring us immediate comfort like drugs, distraction, or drinking destroy us. Choosing discipline leads to joy and joy feeds our soul. Reminiscing about the times we stuck it out and stayed dedicated, feeds us and rejuvenates us.

Hiking changed our lives. Being away from electronics, takes you out of constant stimulation and adds peace to your life. We sit outside more, watch TV less and hike regularly. We sleep outside in our backyard often, just to hear the frogs and crickets or watch for shooting stars. Going through difficult things as a couple forged our bond. Just like in our home life, we fought, made up and grew together.

Ray and I started a private practice in 2002 to work with couples and created a method we call Couples Synergy. We know the way because we both learned how to be healthy after toxic relationships. We work hard on our own relationship every day, and we have witnessed thousands of couples change their own journey. Just like our ultimate hike along the JMT, relationships need the commitment to keep taking another step, going up and over the next pass, and celebrating the mile markers along the way.

Our first relationship is parent/child. Since this is all that we experience, we show up in our adult relationships in these ways, Mother/Son or Father/Daughter. Creating an adult/adult relationship is a skill that needs to be learned, developed and practiced. Just like my husband and I needed to learn survival skills and how to use our equipment to have the confidence to navigate whatever came our way to survive in the mountains.

Fighting well and learning how to heal past hurts so you can grow together, is the most important thing a human being can do. There are important lessons a person learns as a single person but there are also lessons that can only be learned with a partner. We have often been asked, "why don't they teach us this in high school". We don't know why but we are teaching it now and are honored to have witnessed thousands of couples heal and grow.

There is no perfect person out there. What is more important, is to find someone who is willing to work on things and grow with you. We get wounded through relationships and we heal through relationships. The hardest part of working on it, is that we have very few resources to teach us how. So we created a podcast and company to teach people what they can do to create the relationship they've always dreamed of, with the partner they fell in love with.

The key to success: Keep putting one foot in front of the other. It works on mountain tops as well as in relationships.

You can find out more about our hiking adventures on Facebook at "On the Trail with Ray and Jean". In regards to relationships, you can listen to our podcast, "Couples Synergy," where we tackle tough topics and interview couples about their relationships, join us for a weekend intensive and visit our website www.CouplesSynergy.com

Jean Kadkhodaian

Jean Kadkhodaian was born in 1966. She is the fourth of nine children. The most pivotal times of her life were serving in the Army Reserves for 13 years, becoming a single mom, surviving several toxic relationships, marrying Dr. Ray Kadkhodaian and against all odds, creating an amazing partnership.

She enjoys traveling, hiking, painting, motorcycle riding, creating stained glass and caring for her pet stingrays and shark. Her passion for learning and analyzing are the foundations for her success in her own life and the lives of those she helps. One of her favorite quotes by Socrates is "an unexamined life is not worth living". She believes that "An unexamined relationship is not worth suffering". The person who hurts us the most, is the person we love the most. We get wounded through relationships and we can only heal through a relationship, by understanding what it is that our partner has to teach us.

In 2002, Dr. Ray and Jean founded The Lighthouse Emotional Wellness Center, where they successfully created a unique method in working with couples, called "Couples Synergy". As a couple, they not only teach relationship power tools, they lead by example. They have a passion for seeing things from the top, which has brought them to mountain peaks around the world. Dr. Ray and Jean are co-hosts of the Couples Synergy Podcast, where they bring you expert insights into relationships every Monday and interview a couple about their love story every Thursday.

They have two grown sons, Alec and Dinyar, a beautiful daughter-in-law Angela and a therapy dog named Jasmine. In 2018, they started an international company "Couples Synergy" to help people "create the relationship they've always dreamed of, with the partner they fell in love with" through weekend workshops, public speaking and their signature Couple 2 Couple program.

Jean Kadkhodaian
Couples Synergy
3205 North Wilke Road, Suite 112
Arlington Heights, IL 60004
847-253-9769
Jean@LightHouseEmotionalWellness.com
www.CouplesSynergy.com

Sofia Husnain

The Journey of a Thousand Miles...

I remember receiving the phone call from my doctor that the biopsy was positive. It was October 8, 2010. I was twenty years old. I was diagnosed with a condition that I read about in my nursing books. It was a lifelong, chronic, degenerative, debilitating illness with no cure. Time stood still, as I envisioned the next years of my life. Adversities and challenges were old friends. However, this shook me to the core.

You see, childhood wasn't easy. I suppose that's a reality for many people. My story began in the arms of a single mother in a country thousands of miles away, from where women are anything but equal partners in a male dominant society. Women have no rights, no voice, no freedom and no power. Despite these odds, my mother tried to make childhood as safe and fun as possible for her two girls. She hid her sadness, loneliness, despair and abandonment from her husband, with as much strength and vitality as possible. She was, however, only human. Some of my earliest memories have included sharing just a single piece of bread for a meal, doors slamming, loud screaming and hysterical crying every now and then, when my father would visit and hiding and living in constant fear.

As a family, we experienced break-ins, burglary at gunpoint, sexual harassment and physical, verbal and mental abuse. Even in the face of such difficulties, I witnessed my mother stand back up, brush herself off, put a strong face on for her girls and smile. She did this because she knew we needed her. She knew what abandonment meant and that she could not do the same to her girls as their father did. She also knew that without her, a dark, ugly and dangerous world waited for her girls, ready to consume every bit of their existence.

My mother was my first example of a real-life hero. When I was eleven, she made a decision that changed the trajectory of our lives forever. It was a difficult decision. However, it is true what they say, "When you do what is easy, your life will be hard. When you do what is hard, your life will be easy."

Life in America came at a price. The struggle was not over, but we had ample opportunities, that were waiting to be taken by a man or a woman. There was work required, of course. However, the only obstacle between us and the opportunity this time was not tyranny, androcentrism, being the wrong gender or having a lack of experience—but rather our mindset. I quickly learned that in America, in order to build the life of your dreams, you first have to correct your mindset and your attitude. What is behind the eyes, is more powerful than what is in front of them. You must put in the work consistently, as if your life depended on it.

My mother knowingly took on the immense responsibility of starting a brand-new life in an unknown place, fighting for what she believed was a life that could be ours. It was a life that she knew we deserved. The price she paid for working so hard was the time lost with her children. Years have gone by in the blink of an eye, from the time we first entered this country to high school and eventually college graduation. Trading time for money was all my mother knew. Putting food on the table was necessary for survival and building this dream life. To this day, my mother regrets nothing but this.

My mother was not the only one bringing a paycheck home. Because her hourly wages were low, my sister and I had to pick up odd jobs to help pay the bills, as much as possible. I remember having a job as young as thirteen. My sister and I would not participate in sports or any after school activities, because we had to report to work. However, that is not something I regret. It taught me the value of money and savings. Together, the three of us built our dream life. We found happiness in small wins. We were grateful for the little we had, because it was ours and no one could take it away from us.

Going to college and finding a high paying job was non-negotiable. This was, in a way, a tribute from us to our mother for her sacrifices. Having a good work ethic, being grateful for having a job and planning for your dream retirement and life of complete freedom was a topic often talked about at family gatherings. I remember being envious of the elderly finally getting to experience that "freedom". However, it haunted me to think that in order to be completely free, I would have to wait decades. That is if I could even make it that far. I would then only have a few years to enjoy it. Although I had accepted that as my fate, it made me very uneasy every time the thought would appear.

I decided to go to nursing school. To me, it was the perfect marriage of my love for science and a passion for serving my community. After college, I began working as a nurse in the orthopedic unit at the local hospital. I loved my patients but hated the management politics, budget cuts and lay-offs, living in constant fear of being the next one to be let go, being overworked with little staff, having no time for breaks over a 12-14-hour shift, being unappreciated and undermined by doctors with no autonomy and needing the doctor's permission to perform simple tasks. Even after a job well-done, I would be rewarded with a 25 cent raise at the annual employee review, as a thanks from management. Needless to say, I got burned out. It is a joke among nurses that we all have a shelf life.

I went back to school for additional education, with the belief that it would solve the quest of pursuing my true passion. I obtained a Master's Degree in health care administration and started working in the insurance world. I climbed the corporate ladder and had managed a team of about 25 individuals. I was the boss with a lot of responsibility. However, I remember still feeling empty, hollow, fake, going through the motions day after day and knowing deep down that this is not my desired life.

I remember being lost and desperate to find my calling, purpose and true passion. I knew that I loved serving my community. However, I also craved freedom and the ability to make my own decisions about the trajectory of my life. The problem was, I had no idea how to get there. I also knew deep down that needing to wait decades to enjoy a free life was not for me. I knew that working for someone else my whole life, would never lead me to the life of my dreams. I wanted a life of complete and utter freedom. This included freedom of time, freedom of finances, freedom to never wake up to an alarm clock and freedom to do what I want, when I want and with who I want. My mother made sure that we never forgot our past. I dreamed of starting organizations for women back home, including young girls who were searching for their way through life like I was. I knew that such a world existed. I just didn't know how to enter it. I prayed for direction, clarity and a way to find my light to shine on a world filled with darkness.

Did God ever answer a prayer that made you think to yourself and say? "That's not it!". The prayer was answered in the shape of a curveball so scary, that it literally took my breath away. In my journey of soul searching, I hit a rock bottom so low that I thought surely, it can't get any worse than this. However, it actually did. I felt like a lone ship, in the middle of the sea and at the center of a storm.

When I received the devastating news ten years ago, life had almost ended before it even truly began. I was 20 years old and in nursing school. After experiencing some vague symptoms (which I simply disregarded as "stress"), I was diagnosed with a condition that I like to call the big "C". It wasn't cancer. However, it was a lifelong, chronic, degenerative, debilitating illness with no cure, called Crohn's disease. For the following six long years, I was put on multiple fancy Band-Aids (also known as clinical protocols) developed by western medicine and pharmaceutical companies. These Band-Aids cost thousands of dollars, financial and emotional debt, a struggling marriage and an inability to bear children. The combination of these factors caused my life to come to a halt. My life was very dark. It was full of hate, anger, despair, self-loathing and the loss of hope, faith or purpose. I was living my worst nightmare every day, physically, emotionally and financially. After feeling lost and misplaced from my purpose for years, I completely gave up and accepted my circumstances.

The miracle came, to which I replied: "No, Thanks!". A good friend saw my health struggles and introduced me to an unknown territory of functional medicine, also known as holistic and natural medicine. After being broke, tired, miserable and scared for years, I was without a doubt a huge skeptic. This friend was the miracle sent from God. I truly owe my life to her persistence. After turning her down several times, I decided to give in and "give it a try". Approximately six weeks later, I received a phone call from my doctor wanting to know what I was up to. Expecting the worst news, he surprised me by saying that my blood work looked the best that it had in six years. This incident occurred approximately three and a half years ago. I have been in remission ever since. I am not cured and never will be. However, I no longer have the debilitating symptoms of an intense illness, such as draining fatigue, chronic anemia, incapacitating pain, depression and anxiety, multiple food intolerances, frequent trips to the bathroom and repeatedly trying and failing with a variety of remedies to cover up these symptoms.

A major flaw in our medical and nursing school systems is that not enough emphasis is placed on how your body naturally behaves and how to keep that foundation strong. Instead of finding causes for the symptoms, they are masked and covered up for temporary relief. After an extensive self-educating journey on holistic and functional health, I began to expand my reach to many people who I knew were waiting for their own miracles. Over the years, I have helped those with cancer and autoimmune conditions, as well as those suffering from heart disease, diabetes, digestive ailments and even hormonal imbalances which caused stubborn weight gain.

There are always lessons in the past. I am grateful that my father was never a part of my life. It taught me to stand on my own two feet, without ever needing a man. I am grateful for living a life of poverty and submission in my home country. It taught me to never take for granted the wonderful opportunity my mother gave us, by moving to America. I am grateful for my life-long, chronic and debilitating disease. It taught me the value of health and gave me the ability to connect with and resonate with other people's struggles. What I believed were challenges and adversities, were, in fact, the greatest blessings from God. I heard a wonderful quote which said "Life doesn't happen to me. I make life happen." Life begins when you become uncomfortable about your belief systems. When your belief systems change, it is a magic key that unlocks your dreams. These belief systems allow you to consistently work on your identity. Your life is a reflection of your inner identity that must correlate with your conscious mind. This ultimately formulates the vision for your life.

After my belief systems changed, my life took a different turn. I am now in my best physical health. I call myself an entrepreneur and a mother to an eighteen-month-old baby girl. I have financial freedom, which is a reflection of the value my business has brought to others. I have time freedom, thanks to the flexibility of being an entrepreneur. I am a full time, hands-on mom. I get to watch my daughter grow and be fully present in both her life and my own life. I am building my business, expanding and constantly in search of those wanting more from life, I did. As the quote states, "I am a lighthouse, rather than a lifeboat. I do not rescue, but rather help others find their way to shore."

I choose to lead life proactively, not reactively. I pray that my story resonates with you, brings you hope, faith in the future, and gratitude for whatever challenges life throws at you. I love connecting with new people, so please reach out. Success leaves clues. It is up to you to decide how to step into your future. Are you ready for the most exciting rollercoaster ride of your life?

Sofia Husnain

Sofia Husnain is a registered nurse, entrepreneur, speaker and holistic wellness coach. Sofia immigrated to the United States with her older sister and mother at the age of eleven. Always curious and passionate to learn more about the human body, Sofia chose nursing as her career. However, while in nursing school, she was diagnosed with a chronic, debilitating, degenerative and life-long disease, which changed the trajectory of her life forever. After trying and failing many different clinical trials and protocols, the options of continual treatment were quickly fading. The miracle came as her friend – also a nurse - one day introduced her to a system of natural and holistic products. Reluctantly giving holistic medicine a chance, she was amazed at how quickly her body healed from the inside out. Although her illness has no cure, Sofia saw the possibilities and the potential of what educating the community about holistic health can create. Her passion is now to serve and educate her community on their health and body and to empower and equip them with the right tools to get started. She became part of a company called Yoli, which has created thousands of testimonials of men and women getting their life and health back. Sofia focuses on educating others on how the body naturally behaves and how to simply just keep that foundation strong. Her mission is to spread her education and find other "wellness warriors" looking to join her cause. Sofia is married and the mother of an eighteen-month-old baby girl. She enjoys the flexibility, time and financial freedom of being an entrepreneur, as well as the ability to watch her daughter grow and be fully present in her life. Sofia's own personal struggles have allowed her to connect with others on a much deeper level. In hindsight, her lifelong illness is actually her biggest blessing.

Sofia Husnain
Yoli
3546 Ayres Drive
Aurora, IL 60506
630-802-2441
Sofia.Zafar@gmail.com
SHusnain2.Yoli.com

Caryn Kent Dean

Transform Your Story. Transform Your Impact.

I am an introvert. I always have been. It's always there.

I am a creative. I receive great joy when manifesting things.

I am a giver. I have a habit of putting everyone else and everything else first.

I am a dreamer and a realist wrapped up in a single being.

These characteristics have brought wonderful people and experiences into my life.

Throughout my life, I have pursued different interests than most of my peers. This included violin, when everyone else chose flute, swimming instead of softball, Latin instead of French, family and work instead of play, and a favorite book or movie, instead of a party.

I'm a quiet person who prefers to converse one-on-one or in a small group. If someone has so much to say that I can't get a word in, then I have learned to allow them that. If what I have to say is important to them, they will give me an opening. And then they will get to know me.

I have had my ups and downs over the years. Being a sensitive soul has frequently made it difficult to find happiness and belonging.

Because of this, I do doubt myself and the value of my story. However, I think everyone has an important story to tell. I am writing this exactly because it will help someone like me and someone who feels like I do.

Not A Housewife

I had a "normal" suburban, middle-class childhood. I can't say that I ever did anything particularly special or noteworthy. But I had a loving family and got to go on amazing adventures with them. To this day, I love to travel.

My freshman year of high school, I decided I would attend college at Loyola University Chicago and study Latin in the College of Arts and Sciences. I also decided that I would study at the Rome Center in Italy during my sophomore year, for the full year.

I knew only one other person headed to Rome that year. I was terrified. However, I settled in, made friends and traveled to my heart's content.

I took every Etruscan, Greek and Roman art and architecture class available. I decided I wanted to be a Classical Archaeologist and took on a second degree, a Bachelor of Science in Anthropology.

I intended to graduate in four years, so my nose was in a book every second of the next two years. I managed to scrape through with a 3.5-grade point average, which gave me Cum Laude status.

Because of my workload during my senior year, I held off on applying for doctoral programs in Classical Archaeology until the fall. I ended up without a doctoral program, however. There weren't many programs and the competition was fierce for the few openings in them.

That led me to apply for a research position in a law firm. I'd worked in libraries and was comfortable with the idea of that work.

I eventually applied for a local Master of Library and Information Science program. I worked full-time and studied full-time, paying my own way and completing my degree in just two years.

Up until this point, my adult life had been spent studying and working. I had a few friends. I went out with them occasionally, but it was nothing extraordinary.

While working on my Master Degree at Rosary College, I met the founder of a software company in the library marketplace. They needed a Proposal Writer and I got the job. I had absolutely no idea what I was getting into.

That was now more than 20 years ago. That company taught me many hard-won lessons. I met so many amazing people. It definitely set me on a path that I never imagined for myself.

I learned that I was actually really good at writing business proposals. I was also good at process improvement and implementing programs.

I also met the love of my life there. We were married in 2002, spent a few years working and going on amazing adventures. We brought three beautiful children into the world. I had the great honor of being their full-time caregiver for ten years.

Being a parent is hard. We had our first child in 2005, the second in 2007 and the third in 2009. Three children, four and under, are a handful! Once our youngest came along, our family felt complete.

The kids grew up. One by one, they started school and activities. My husband supported us wonderfully and still has a great career. He was away from home 12 hours most days. While I did make a few friends among the parents, I felt isolated.

In 2014, our youngest was ready for kindergarten. We'd just moved to a dream home. It made sense for me to return to work. I looked at job ads and wondered what I would do.

A former colleague, whom I'd helped develop in her career in business proposals, reached out to me one day. She asked if I knew anyone who might be looking for a Proposal Writer position. I responded that I might be.

She was surprised, but I applied. The interview process went well. She supported me throughout. I think the recruiter was very skeptical about my technology skills. After all, it had been 10 years! How could he possibly think I'd know how to use modern office technology? It was pretty amusing.

Their interview process took several months. The week before they made a job offer, a recruiter from another company reached out to me. I had three phone screens and one in-person interview with the team within a week. They sent me a job offer right away.

In the end, I had two job offers and chose the opportunity that felt best. I was elated and chose to work with my former colleague. I joined the company at a lower level than my last professional position. I felt it was exactly right for balancing work and family.

I was a quick learner and had a positive impact on the team quickly. I definitely had to get used to instant messaging and Skype meetings. After a while, I realized that the position and company were not the right fit for me.

Looking back, there were a few catalysts. My career ambition and passion for learning had kicked back into gear. I didn't feel like I fit with the team or organization. And I was beginning to struggle with balance.

Not two years into that position, I saw that the other company that had offered me a position was looking for Proposal Managers. I refreshed my resume and sent it off to the recruiter I had worked with previously.

The process went quickly again. I interviewed the team as carefully as they interviewed me. The next month, I was in the new role. It seemed like the perfect fit!

There was a very steep learning curve, but I was up for the challenge. Everything was going my way. I learned their complex processes and policies quickly. I was also able to work from home three days a week, once fully trained.

I was polite, worked hard, stepped up for special projects and got to know the team. I felt that I was making a difference.

However, I was drowning. I was effective in my work and assigned a heavy workload. I tried to push back but frequently wasn't successful.

I was stressed and frequently wearing too many hats at once. I remember one summer day when I was working from home. The nanny texted me a question and was having trouble with the kids fighting, my husband walked into the office to ask a question and my manager was trying to call—all in the space of a couple of minutes!

At one point, I ended up very sick and in immediate care on intravenous antibiotics. I had a deadline, though, so I pushed through once back home and got the work done.

A senior colleague left the team shortly after that. I was suddenly being assigned the highest-profile deals that required executive approvals. The pressure was even more intense.

Just a year into the position, I realized that the team approach to proposals that I had been led to expect based on my careful questioning during interviews, just wasn't there. I was giving up vacations and holiday time due to work assignments.

I was the only woman on that team based in that office with young children at home. And my manager would frequently tell me, "You are not a housewife."

It was just before Christmas that I hit my limit. My dad needed surgery in January. He had experienced severe complications after previous surgeries, and I was worried. I felt that I needed to be in the hospital with him and I might even need to take a week or two off.

My boss told me I would not be allowed to take time off because, "You are not a housewife."

I was offended, angry and done. Over the holidays, I told my husband I would need to leave corporate. He was amazing and supportive. I was terrified and hopeful, all at once.

I muddled through the next six months. My last day as an employee was June 1, 2018.

During that time, I realized that I am unemployable.

Learning Who I Am

During my time with my last employer, my boss frequently mentioned how lucky we were to have our jobs. She'd tell us how companies were firing their entire proposal teams and hiring contractors. What she didn't know, was that companies were reaching out to me to see if I was open to contract work.

I was back in corporate for less than four years. I went back because that's what people do. They work to support their families. I wanted to support my family, too.

But doing it the way everyone else does never felt right.

I think God was trying to tell me that the whole time. He put out so many signs.

Today I am an entrepreneur. I have been for a year now. It absolutely has its challenges and I still have frustrating days.

That being said, it's the best choice I'd made for *me* in a very long time.

I have the honor of working with clients who choose me. I choose when I work and get to pour creativity into my work in and on my business. I also hustle every day to make this dream a reality.

Are you trying to fit into a life and balance that doesn't feel right? Does everything look perfect on paper? Are you completely exhausted, empty and anxious?

Are you missing out on experiences? Will you regret missing them later on? Have you lost you?

If so, I encourage you to search your soul. Watch for the signs. Listen to your gut. Figure out what it is that will fulfill you and bring you a happy life.

As a librarian in training only, I advise you to do your research. Find a business and mindset coach. It turns out that my business coach is helping me with both. I didn't realize how much work I had and still have to do on mindset.

The greatest blessing of entrepreneurship has been that I feel isolated less frequently. I've met so many other creative and sensitive souls on their version of this path. I am better because of these relationships.

Nothing is perfect. I am the ultimate work in progress. Entrepreneurship is enabling my best version of life. I am becoming a better wife, mother and human. My time and energy on this earth will have a bigger impact.

I am grateful for the opportunity to transform my clients' proposal stories, so that they can have a bigger impact.

Are you an introvert, creative, giver who feels out of balance, although everything looks perfect on paper, too?

There is hope. The answer is within you. I believe in you.

Caryn Kent Dean

Caryn Kent Dean is an introvert, creative and sensitive entrepreneur. She grew up in La Grange Park, IL and received her B.A., Classics and B.S., Anthropology, both Cum Laude, from Loyola University Chicago. She is an alum of the 1999–2000 class that studied at Loyola's John Felice Rome Center. In 1997, she completed her Master of Library and Information Science at Rosary College (now Dominican University) Circumstances after library school led to her introduction to the work of a proposal professional. After six years and a variety of roles, including as a software company's first Proposal Manager, Caryn decided to pursue other interests.

She married Corey Dean in 2002. They lived in Chicago and then moved to Villa Park, Illinois, in 2006. As children came along, she had the great honor of being a full- time mom for ten years. She returned to the corporate world in another proposal-related position, when her youngest entered full-day kindergarten. Four years and two companies later, Caryn was inspired to leave corporate and become an entrepreneur.

In 2018, Caryn founded Once Upon an RFP, where they transform clients' proposal stories to win the best business and make a bigger impact. You'll now find Caryn enjoying her work with clients, as well as the creative and intellectual challenges of business ownership.

The Association of Proposal Management Professionals (APMP) recognized Caryn with Foundation Certification in 2016. In May 2019, APMP recognized Caryn with Practitioner Certification. To date, only 1,127 professionals around the world have been recognized at this level.

In addition to professional certification through APMP, on September 19, 2019, the Greater Midwest Chapter recognized Caryn as 2019 Member of the Year. She was nominated for spearheading the effort to create a Virtual Networking Group to connect proposal consultants with their peers and provide relevant programs and support.

When Caryn's not working with clients or on her business, you'll find her with whom she loves best, her husband, kids, and sweet puppy, Scout.

Caryn Kent Dean
Once Upon an RFP LLC
1210 S. Wayside Drive
Villa Park, IL 60181
312-388-0091
Caryn@OnceUponanRFP.com
www.OnceUponanRFP.com

Amanda Jean Jarratt

Only the Strong Survive

Have you ever wondered how some people can survive an obstacle, yet another person will fail at the same challenge? Does it have to do with a person's background? Could it be that they were born stubborn? Well, for me, I believe it has to do with inner strength, pride, ego and self-motivation.

When I was a small child, I would often hear my mother say," Only the Strong Survive". It would typically be said in a conversation pertaining to some sort of trouble. I never knew what it really meant, until I became older.

Like most teens, I began searching for who I was and how I could fit in. I found myself dating someone much older, looking for acceptance, love and attention. At the age of 16, I had my first child. I was only a child myself. My family was embarrassed, ashamed and disappointed. I was in shock and didn't know what to do. I was in a relationship that was mentally, verbally and physically abusive. Have you ever been in a situation and didn't know how to get out of it? I wanted to immediately give up. However, something in my spirit whispered, "Only the Strong Survive". I pressed forward, believing that God would bring me out. Although everyone else gave up on me and counted me out, God said, "He would never leave me or forsake me". I trusted him and had faith that he would work it all out.

At the age of 18, I found myself in another relationship and pregnant with my second child. You're probably saying, "Oh my God, not again". Well, this relationship wasn't so bad. I was now working and had my own home and vehicle. My partner and I lived together and shared all of the responsibilities, which made things a lot easier. Things were going pretty good for a while, until there was a misunderstanding. Have you ever lost a career, spouse, friendship or family member over a misunderstanding? You would think that it could be easily resolved, right? In this case, the misunderstanding began to involve others. It eventually became overwhelming and things escalated to a point, where it was too far out of control.

So, here I was again. I was all alone with two small children. I had been through many things at an early age. I felt rejected, betrayed and unworthy. I was broken and scarred. It appeared that favor wasn't on my side. If I never wanted to give up before, I certainly wanted to give up now. In that moment, I heard a small whisper, "Only the Strong Survive".

So, what did I do? I decided to be a survivor and not a victim. So What? I'm a single mother with no college education and no support. I will never forget that moment. This is because it was the exact moment when my life changed forever. I looked at my two sons, as we sat in the dark. I said, "I will survive for you". I decided that day, I would never let my mishaps or misfortunes be a crutch but rather my motivation.

Do you know that everything is a process? Plans, actions and strategies must be in place in order to accomplish goals and visions. I learned quickly that if I wanted to prove to myself or anyone else I was not a victim, but a survivor, that I needed to have a plan. I sat down, wrote out a list of what I wanted to do, who I wanted to become and how I could make it happen. I kept that list folded in my bible. I would check things off, as I achieved them. I prayed over that list every day.

Someone once said, "It doesn't matter how you start but it is how you finish". That statement hit home for me. I often tell others the same thing, because we sometimes feel because we are in a mess, that we have to stay in a mess. I started off very young, timid, shy, with a lack of education and low self-esteem. I had no support and no motivation. However, I kept hearing a whisper that reminded me that it didn't have to end like this. That whisper kept me going. Was the whisper my conscience, an angel, or was it God? Whoever or whatever it was, I'm very thankful.

Have you ever lost something that you depended on to survive? It was hard enough being a single mother of two and working full-time. I had the audacity to go back to school full-time. After years of sacrifice and sleepless nights, I had finally gotten to a position in my life financially that I was no longer stressed out and worried. I was finally able to pay my bills on time, take a vacation, shop without having an anxiety attack and most importantly, SAVE money. Life was amazing. I had a new car, a new home and a promotion at work. Life was great.

Has one event in your life ever changed your entire life? I went to work bright and early as usual. It was a super busy morning. My employees and I were rushing around and serving our guests. Then BOOM in the blink of an eye, my life changed. I didn't even know it. One of my employees made a sudden turn and stepped on my left foot. It caused me to lose my balance and almost fall. Everything happened very fast. I was in shock, but the business must go on. As business began to slow down and the adrenaline rush came to a crash, I realized that my foot really hurt. I took off my shoe and sock, to see that my foot had turned blue and purple. I ended up going to the doctor and had to leave work and go on worker's compensation. I had to go through months of physical therapy, weight gain and disappointment. I lost the one thing that I depended on to survive, my CAREER. I panicked not knowing what to do and how I would survive. My children came to my mind immediately. How would I pay my bills? Would I lose my home? Would I lose my vehicles? Would I be able to find a new job? I was depressed for months and didn't want to leave my home. I realized that my faith was being tested. What did I do? How did I overcome my anxiety and depression? Did I lose the material things that I was worried about?

No, I didn't lose my home or cars that I had worked so hard for. I snapped out of the anxiety/depression mode rather quickly, because I remembered "Only the Strong Survive". I realized that my job was just a job. It wasn't the job that was so important and full of worth and value. It was me that was important and valuable. I also realized how many people were depending on me. It wasn't just my kids. I decided to use what happened to me to make me stronger, because only the strong will survive. I finished my Master's Degree in business and went to Real Estate school.

I decided that it was okay to change career paths, because it didn't matter what the job was. I was going to make the job worth having. I did a lot of praying and meditating. I started writing out my vision. As the bible says, "write your vision and make it plain". I began to pray about my purpose and realized that God took me through the devastation, just to get me to the manifestation. You can't get caught up in anger, anxiety and depression, when things don't go your way. You have to sit still, pray about it and see what the lesson was in that scenario. I chose not to sit or pray for sympathy. I chose to stop throwing myself a pity party. Why? It was because it wasn't paying my bills and it wasn't fulfilling my purpose. I had to shake it off. When I say that, I mean, shake off the hurt, shake off the pride, shake off the ego and shake off ME. We can sometimes block our own blessing. I decided I didn't want to do that. I started writing affirmations on my mirror. I wrote out all my goals on post-it notes and hung them around my bed frame and my television screen. I was determined that the only thing I would breathe, see and say were positive things. That is when life began to change for me. When I started seeing life from a different perspective, my faith became stronger and I became wiser.

Today, at the age of 35, I am still a single mother of two. However, I do have my Master's Degree in business. I hold my North Carolina Real Estate License. I am also the very proud owner of His Chosen Investment Group LLC. I work diligently in the community trying to help others like ME. I work hard to put together events that allow my business to give in multiple ways, such as providing school supplies and backpacks to children in the community, supporting single moms and supplying food to the homeless. I have a passion for mentoring, educating and guiding individuals in the direction of success. My heart goes out to single women, especially with children. I know how it feels to not know what to do, to not have enough and to not think that you're good enough. I have been told many times that I am a NOBODY who would NEVER amount to anything. How did I get over that fear? How did I push past the negative thoughts? How was I able to use the negative energy and turn it into positivity? How could I possibly help others overcome what I've experienced? How is it even possible for me to tell others about the embarrassing moments of my life?

Who would have thought that a young teenage mother who was scarred, broken, scared and confused with no plans and no support, would ever become anything? Statistics counted me out. Family and friends counted me out. At one point, I counted myself out. Have you ever counted yourself out? Life can be hard. We are all dealt a different hand. However, I believe it is how you play that hand. I like to look at the glass as half full, instead of half empty. It can be hard to do but it provides a positive insight.

If I had to give you a formula of how to overcome and beat statistics, it would be simply to believe in yourself. All the odds were against me, or at least I thought they were. My mistakes may have held me back and caused me to not live my original dream. However, if you only have one dream, you're really not a dreamer. I learned how to survive, how to make things work and how to balance life. How did I learn to do that? My only fear was FAILURE. I guess you could say that failure was my remedy. Failure was my motivation. Failure is why I kept going. Failure and I never got along. I vowed to myself that no matter what happened in life, failure was not an option. It started with motivation. My children were my motivation. They then became my drive and focus that kept me on the path to success. Have you ever wanted to prove someone wrong? My entire life has proven several people wrong. I am not saying that proving people wrong should be your motto. However, it should be whatever works for you. It worked for me. I found that praying, trusting and believing that God had more for me, was the foundation of it all. When you feel like giving up and you can't go on, I will be that whisper in your ear telling you, "Only the Strong Survive".

Amanda Jean Jarratt

Amanda Jarratt was born in Petersburg, Virginia in 1984. She grew up in a small town, where she loved to ride bikes, run track and sing songs. Her imagination was bigger than anyone could ever believe, and her spirit was filled with love, care and passion for people. At a young age, she became a believer in Christ and her footsteps have never been the same. She made many mistakes, but she fell back on her spiritual beliefs and rose again.

Amanda has two sons, who are 17 and 18 years old. She holds an MBA in Business Administration and Human Resource Management. She has operated multi-million dollar companies, holds her North Carolina Real Estate license and is part owner of a professional cleaning company.

Her knowledge, wisdom and vision are well above-average. Amanda's best asset is giving back to others. Her motto is "Give and it shall come back to you". She believes in mentoring, educating and spreading knowledge to the community.

Amanda has decided to step out on faith, as she has created a faith-based business of investing. Her vision for this company is far beyond what any individual could ever imagine. She believes that it starts with a solid foundation. She has chosen individuals who support her vision. She teaches them individually and guides them in what she calls a "massive movement". Her passion and purpose on earth is to help build, guide and push others into success. Therefore, His Chosen Investment Group was established by the faith of a mustard seed.

Amanda Jean Jarratt

His Chosen Investment Group LLC

3745 Landshire View Lane

Raleigh, NC 27616

919-210-2304

AJarratt1357@gmail.com

www.HisChosenInvestmentGroup.com

Terri Howard

The Struggle is Over

My story begins in Savannah, Georgia, where my parents met and fell deeply in love. My mom, Barbara, was only 18 years old and my dad, Harold, was 20 years old. My dad would leave to go to the Marines, soon after the marriage. Barbara whose own dad was controlling and never allowed her to have a voice, soon found out she had married a man who was both controlling and would silence her even more than her dad. In those days, many men controlled the home and the women had to learn to live with it. There was not much support for women who did not want to go along to get along. Women did not realize that they were allowed to own their own home, have their own credit card or put utilities in their names. Women were expected to leave their dad's home and get married. This was one of the reasons for my mom getting married at such an early age.

My mom went into nursing and my dad became a postal worker. I was born Terri Howard, on June 29, 1957, in Savannah, Georgia, I was the middle child to this Christian, middle class, seemingly functional family. I was bequeathed with tremendous responsibility and even more, when my younger sister was born. I never felt like I had a childhood. My older brother and I found ourselves not only being supportive of our co-dependent mother but in the middle of many arguments between our mom and dad. Life in the sixties was a lot different than today. Parents loved their children, but many felt that children were only to be seen and not to be heard. I always had the feeling that I did not fit in; at home or at school. My mom and dad just seemed to make demands on me and never gave me much attention. I never had the nerve to ask why I was not allowed to say what I was thinking. I would have screamed at the top of my lungs, "I'm your daughter. I have feelings and I need more than I am getting from you." Would they have even heard me? I never felt like I had my own voice. Did my mom even love me and did she know I wanted to be closer to her? Was I invisible to her? I went through my entire childhood feeling like I was alone.

There was one angel in my life. She was my grandmother, Ella Mae Capers. My grandmother was one of eighteen children. She was a beautiful woman. She was a full Cherokee Indian with pure black, long and wavy hair. Her parents allowed the pastor and his wife to raise my grandmother. She often spoke on how the pastor's wife dressed her like a princess. At their home, she was treated like Cinderella. She did all the cleaning, washing and cooking. At an early age, she ran away and landed in Savannah, Georgia. My grandfather fell madly in love with her. They married and had four children. My grandmother was never around her siblings very much. Therefore, like me, she didn't feel connected. I do not think she ever understood her childhood. One day she made the decision not to carry the victim sign anymore. Amazingly, she learned to love from a hurt place.

She loved her grandchildren and her great-grandchildren. My brother and I were her first grandchildren. We always knew she loved us. Since my mom worked many shifts as a nurse, we were left with our grandmother many days and nights. She talked to us all the time, telling us the stories of her life. She was the first adult to play games and just have fun with us. She always took us to church and taught us about God's love. The meals she cooked will stay in our memories for the rest of our lives. My grandmother lived until she was 100 years old. I can't ever remember her saying a bad word or being judgmental of anyone. She loved the Lord with all her heart and had so much faith. I always told her I just wanted to be half the woman that she was. My grandmother would say, "You already are". I really did not understand what she meant until years later. I have always aspired to be a caring person, just like my grandmother.

My family would move from Savannah to New York City. The disagreements became more and more violent between my parents. The atmosphere in our home became very hostile. We never knew what to expect from day to day. I was a child watching my family breakdown. It took years to fight my way through all those feelings. I was looking for my mom to nurture and love me. I did not understand that she just did not have anything to give. She was in survival mode and was doing everything she knew how to raise her children. She was working too many hours to keep a roof over our heads and food in the refrigerator.

Soon after my graduation from high school, my mom left my dad. She took my younger sister and moved back to Savannah. My brother and I stayed in New York City and continued to raise ourselves. Many people were moving out west to the wonderful sunshine and beaches. My brother decided to make the move to California. I understood why he wanted to move. However, I really felt alone. I still had my dreams that God had put in my heart years ago (to one day help people). The fact that my mom, sister and brother were gone made me think; maybe I did not belong to this family. Maybe it was a big mistake. Being homesick for my family and not wanting them to know I could not take care of myself, I married and had my daughter, La Shawn. She was born on March 4th, 1978 in New York City. I knew she was a gift from God and a turning point in my life. That feeling did not last long. Once again, I was in an abusive, dysfunctional family. Within 18 months of this marriage, God provided me with the strength to realize He did not give me this gift of life to be in a relationship that would destroy me and my daughter. My life with my childhood flashed in my mind and I knew I had to pack my little girl up and get out of New York City.

My daughter and I would make one of our first of many geographical moves and went to Georgia. This was the beginning of my downward spiral into darkness and into a world, I did not think I could control. Spinning, Spinning, and Spinning, bound by invisible chains and losing myself.

La Shawn was a loving little girl. She always gave me a wonderful smile. It would often jolt me back into reality. However, the addiction was much stronger than her love (so I thought). At least that's what it seemed like, back in those days. We moved from Georgia to California, to Arizona.

Continuously indulging in drugs, not always having our own place, I always had a job(s). Even when I was deep in my addiction, I worked two jobs for over twenty years. I was not broke but there were many times I could not afford my rent, utilities, childcare, and food. Something inside of me would not let me settle for life in a shelter. I could not bring myself to take my little girl to an unsafe, unclean place. By the grace of God, we were never homeless and never lived in a shelter. The assistance might not have come when I wanted it to come, but it always came in time. I believe it was the prayers of my grandmother that always sent someone to help us out.

La Shawn became pregnant with Franklin Lee Wright, at the young age of sixteen. Franklin gave me the reason to live, to get my life back on track. We all left Phoenix and moved to Charlotte, NC. where we have lived for the last 21 years. On November 30, 1998, I was on the road to recovery. Two years later, La Shawn would also be on her road to recovery.

After all the moving from state to state, going through a divorce and being addicted, I had lost myself. I had forgotten my dreams. I realized I never was privy to having a protector or having anyone that stood up for me. I had always tried to take care of my daughter and her son. As a result, I sometimes forgot to take care of myself. One day I remembered that God had never left my side. He was my protector, and he always brought a kind person at the right time to help us out. I was able to lift my head a little higher and remembered that His grace and mercy had kept us through all those difficult times. Through God's love and mercy, due to my hard work two years into recovery, I was able to dream again. I remembered dreaming of being self-sufficient and self-supportive. I wanted to be tenacious enough to help others who just needed the resources to succeed.

Still not feeling smart enough, I enrolled in a Christian college. I was able to receive my Associates, Bachelors, and Master degrees. I majored in Organizational Leadership and became a leader who was able to equip others to become leaders. I knew I did not want to make my life in corporate America, so I started my own non-profit, Home for Heroes. I wanted to be a servant leader to others. I didn't have the money, but I found resources to get started. I had volunteers that worked at sporting events to bring in the initial funding.

In November 2010, Home for Heroes opened its first home in Charlotte, NC. It provided female veterans with clean, affordable and safe living spaces. This gave them an opportunity to resurrect their lives. In California, years ago, I was able to find a place like this for my daughter and me. I was working over forty hours a week. However, I did not have enough money to pay my rent, utilities, childcare, and food. This concept resonated with me to create my non-profit. When regular people fall down at times in their life, they just need a little help to regain their lives. It is almost impossible to get yourself together, without having your basic needs met. It means so much to get help, without losing your self-respect.

My life is now much more than I could ever imagine. I came from no self-esteem, no voice and unable to even hold my head up most of the time. Today, I am very grateful for who I am and the person I have become. I was able to help my daughter become the beautiful woman she is today. The daughter (that never wanted to be like her mom), is eagerly running A Place for Heroes that helps house more than 50 vets (females and males) and families.

My greatest achievement is now having my daughter by my side on this journey. It is a loving example of a mother and daughter's love. Some years ago, my daughter, my grandson and I made a family pact, "that no matter what we will stick by each other, through the good times and bad times". I now have that family I was looking for many years ago. I am becoming the woman that my grandmother said I was. I am now walking into the legacy that I want to leave my great-grandchildren, Kayceon, Kennedi and Noland.

"No matter what life gives you, you do not have to become the victim of your circumstances. Keep the faith, stay focused through all things good or bad". If they get nothing else from their great grandmother's story, I want each of them to know to trust in God and continue to always do the best you can do.

Lastly, I thank God for my grandmother, Ella Mae, who was truly a phenomenal woman and a true blessing to my family.

Terri Howard

Terri Howard was born on June 29, 1957, in Savannah, Georgia, to Barbara (nurse) and Harold (postal worker). She was the middle child of a Christian, middle class and seemingly functional family. She never felt like she had a childhood, since she was given the responsibility of caring for her younger sister at an early age. Terri and her older brother found themselves not only being supportive of their co-dependent mother but were in the middle of many abusive attacks to their mother by their father.

Terri and her family moved to New York. Soon after her graduation, her mom left her dad and took the younger sister with her back to Savannah, her brother soon moved to California and Terri was left alone to raise herself. Terri felt totally alone again, with the exception of the dreams that God had put in her heart to one day be able to help people.

She then got married and had her only child. However, once again, she was in an abusive and dysfunctional family. Within 18 months, God gave her the strength to take her daughter and move to Georgia. This was the beginning of her downward spiral into darkness, where she indulged in drugs.

On November 30, 1998, while on the road to recovery, she started her new journey. However, Terri had forgotten her dreams. Through God's love and her hard work, two years into recovery, she started to dream again. God gave her the vision to help those like herself, who needed a hand up and not a handout.

Still not feeling adequate enough, she enrolled in a Christian College and majored in Organizational Leadership. She knew she didn't want to make her life in Corporate America, so she started her own non-profit, Home for Heroes. She is dedicated in her commitment, to providing a safe place for our heroes' veterans with clean and safe living spaces. This will give them an opportunity to resurrect their lives.

In November 2010, Home for Heroes opened their first home in Charlotte, N.C. Today, her daughter (who never wanted to be like her mom), is eagerly running A Place for Heroes that helps house more than 50 vets (female and male) and their families.

Terri feels her greatest achievement today is having her daughter by her side on this journey. They are both a loving example of mother and daughter love.

Terri Howard

A Place for Heroes

744 Seigle Point Drive

Charlotte, NC 28204

704-499-0059

Howard.Terri7@gmail.com

www.APlaceforHeroes.org

Kristin Decker

Fearfully & Wonderfully Made

"Kristin, if I looked like you, I would kill myself." "Kristin, you are ugly." "Kristin, you are fat."

I heard those comments from sixth grade all the way through my senior year in high school. How could I believe I was anything but when I heard those things constantly for seven years?

"You have been assigned this mountain, so that you can show others it can be moved"—Mel Robbins. We all have mountains in our life that we have conquered, that we are currently conquering, and that we will conquer within our lifetime. The trouble with these mountains is that we are so afraid to let other people know we are climbing them. Why is that? Why are we so afraid to let people see us as vulnerable?

How many times have you shared your hard times or the mountains you have climbed to get to where you are today? What if everyone shared their struggles? The scary times they stood at the bottom of the mountain, questioning if they could make it to the top or not. What if we grabbed hands with someone who was at the bottom of the same mountain we climbed and became that one person they needed to let them know they are not alone? What if everyone were open and vulnerable about the mountains they faced, so other people could see them as a sign of hope? Well, here is my mountain…

Beginning in the sixth grade, I was bullied and harassed relentlessly. Two girls created a book about me with comments about how ugly and fat I was. They then posted things from the book online for everyone to read.

I convinced myself that middle school was going to be different, as I prayed the bullying would stop. In eighth grade, things escalated; kids yelled in the hallway that I was ugly and fat. They sent surveys around asking if their friends agreed with that statement. Not only was I bullied in school, but my peers in confirmation class did it too. I became severely depressed and anorexic.

I prayed that the bullying would stop when I started high school. Well, it didn't. During my freshman and sophomore years, my depression and eating disorder worsened. That's when the thoughts of suicide and self-harm started. Adults were no different. A teacher even bullied me. One day when I was walking to take a picture with some friends, this teacher said, "Kristin you know I don't like you, but it's only because you aren't a size 0 and on the cheerleading team." I was a three-sport athlete, my first two years of high school. Why wasn't I enough?

Kids continued picking on me. They compared me to a Chuckie doll and sent my first-grade picture around the school with a note saying, *ugly then, ugly now.* Kids stuck gum in my hair and threw trash at me, telling me they thought I was the trash can. I was grabbing food in the cafeteria one day and my best friend yelled out, "Kristin why are you getting that? You are already fat!" If your best friend makes comments like that or does not stick up for you, they are not your true friend.

They say laughter is the best medicine, but what if every time you laughed, you heard someone yell out, "You sound like a hyena." I spent most nights crying in my bed, wishing that I was dead.

The summer after my sophomore year, I was hospitalized for my eating disorder and suicidal thoughts. The doctors told my parents that I should transfer out of my high school and get help. They said if I didn't, in two months, when we would normally be shopping for my homecoming dress, my parents would be picking out my funeral outfit.

After I was discharged, my parents suggested that I talk with Matt, the youth pastor at my church. At the time, he had been diagnosed with cancer. I shared my story with him, crying the entire time. I asked him, "Why me? Why was I going through this? Is there hope for me?" He looked at me and asked, "Why him, why cancer?" At that moment, I realized I was not alone in my suffering and questioning. Matt became the light for me, as I worked to get myself out of the dark tunnel that engulfed me. He was always there to listen to me and help me on my way to recovery.

I had to re-teach myself how to eat and find different ways to cope, if the bullying were to continue. It took work to get myself out of my severe depression. However, the most important step in my recovery that the doctors told me I needed to do, was to transfer high schools. I met with the principal at my current high school to transfer me to a different school. I changed high schools for my junior and senior years. I walked into my new school, praying that it would be different.

There was no bullying for the first few months of school, until I went on a date with this guy. While driving in the car, he reached over, grabbed my chest, and made a sexual comment. After that happened I felt so violated, I texted a friend to call me to tell me she had a family emergency. She called and I told my date I needed to go home. He dropped me off.

The next day, I started receiving harassing text messages from the guy's friends. They called me names and told me what a horrible person I was for leaving the date early. His friends made oinking and gagging noises, as I walked by. I was then cyberbullied by people who started a forum online for the sole purpose of making fun of me.

One night I received a sexually harassing text message from an unknown number. I was babysitting for a family, whose husband worked for the police department. I read the message and began to cry. The child I was watching ran and got her mom. I showed her the text message and she called her husband, who told us we needed to go to the police station and report it. The two kids who sent the text message were issued a restraining order to stay away from me.

I felt good for finally standing up for myself. Where was this power coming from? My good feelings were short-lived. The next day at school, the kids who got in trouble with the police told their friends what happened. Once people heard, I started receiving harassing text messages from unknown numbers. Some of them included death threats. It was all because I just stood up for myself.

Later that day, someone followed me into the bathroom. They grabbed me and threw me against the bathroom wall, threatening, "If you ever pick your head up again in the hall or go to the police, I will kill you."

I immediately went to the school administration. I was told, "It's OK that she said and did that to you, because she had a rough upbringing."

School was a scary place for me. I was terrified that if I picked my head up in the hall, someone was going to kill me. Thankfully, I had a teacher who allowed me to hang in her classroom during passing periods, when I felt unsafe.

Once I graduated from high school, I never looked back. Since being hospitalized, I have been in remission from my eating disorder, suicidal thoughts, and depression for over 10 years now. That is something that I never thought I would be able to say.

During the darkest moment of my life when I wasn't sure if I could overcome my eating disorder, depression and suicidal thoughts and when I didn't think there was hope for me anymore, Matt was there for me. He let me know that it is okay to question hope. He also showed me that this journey in my story is temporary. However, it taught me a lot. It taught me that I can live freely for people and serve them without worrying about myself or what other people think of me.

I now live my life without apology and in celebration of who God made me to be and look like. I encourage you to do the same, no matter where you are on the mountain you are climbing.

Your identity is **not** defined by your appearance. It is **not** defined by what other people say about you and it is **not** defined by how we view ourselves. God created every single one of us in His perfect image. Our worth is found in Him, not what others say about us. It can be very hard to believe that, especially if you hear something negative about yourself repeatedly. Here is what you need to remind yourself of DAILY, **you are fearfully and wonderfully made**. Society makes it hard for us to believe that, especially when they tell us we need to look and act a certain way. I am encouraging you to **STOP** listening to everyone else. Live your life without apology and in celebration of who **YOU** are. Stop conforming to what the world tells you to be. Instead, **YOU** should be the beautiful you.

What an incredible world it could be, if we all first love ourselves and everyone around us, even those who are "different" than us. We are all unique in our own ways. It is time we live our life embracing every part of what makes us, us. The world needs "insert your name." Now, go back and read that sentence with your name in it again. Now it's time to live your life, without apology.

You can use your story to change the world.

Matt had a major impact on my life for two years before he passed away from his battle with multiple myeloma. My final goodbye with Matt is still one of the hardest things that I have ever had to do. However, it still inspires me to use my story and his influence to change the world, the way that he changed my life. Three years after Matt passed away, I ran 4,000 miles across America from San Francisco, California to Baltimore, Maryland for young adults battling cancer. I ran my miles in his memory. It was important that I share my story how of someone came into my life and changed it during the time the doctors predicted I'd be dead.

We all have our mountain. Whatever that is, it does not define who we are. In fact, our mountain experience can bring hope to others, who are walking a similar journey. I am not defined by what people said about me, nor am I defined by those years I battled an eating disorder, depression, and suicidal thoughts. The same thing is true for you. What you are battling right now, or what you have battled does **not** define you. Sharing our story can be a light to someone who is walking the same path. You can show people that you have made it through and that you are on the side of recovery.

I will be the first person to stand up and say I have been bullied. Because of what kids and adults said and did to me, I battled an eating disorder, depression, suicidal thoughts, and body dysmorphic. However, I have walked through it and I am on the side of recovery. I know that I am defined by one person and one person only. Let me help you carry those bags on your similar journey and help you walk over this mountain that I have climbed before.

What mountain have you climbed that you can now help someone reach the top of? Whatever that mountain is, share your story and be that light for someone, so they know they are not alone. Make it your mission to leave your sparkle in someone's life.

If you would like to partner together to have me speak to the kids close to your heart and to students on the message of bullying prevention and leaving your sparkle, please reach out at www.kdmotivates.com.

Kristin Decker

Kristin Decker inspires audiences everywhere to affect social change. Her passion for community engagement began when she ran 4,000 miles across the United States for young adults battling cancer. She ran in memory of her friend Matthew Peterson, who passed away after a battle with multiple myeloma. Matt's friendship is a constant inspiration in her life. In one of his final letters to her, he wrote: "You will touch lives". Kristin considers this to be her life's motto, and she applies this message to her volunteering efforts. A project that is close to Kristin's heart is Urban Bicycle Food Ministry (UBFM). Individuals involved with this project deliver food and necessities to people affected by homelessness, and they do so through cycling. Not only does UBFM give Kristin an opportunity to give back but being involved with UBFM also helped Kristin to overcome her fear of cycling. She is so passionate about the mission that she carried it with her to her new home: Kristin is the Founder of

UBFM Colorado Springs! For Kristin, facing her fear inspired her to seek new experiences that initially seemed intimidating, and doing so has had a profound impact on her life. She recently spoke to 25,000 high school students about her life-threatening experience with bullying and mental health. She has received very positive feedback about her speech, and she plans to continue sharing her thoughts about bullying and mental health across the country. Kristin earned a master's degree in social work from the University of Memphis. When she isn't affecting social change through volunteering, speaking, and working her daily profession, she enjoys outdoor activities and hanging out with loved ones. For Kristin, leaving her unmistakable sparkle with everyone she meets is an important, lifelong endeavor that she hopes to fulfill every day.

Kristin Decker
224-406-0737
kristin@kdmotivates.com
www.kdmotivates.com

Jenny Bergold

One Year

Eight years ago, I was walking with my son, Michael, feeling particularly sad. Sensing me, he pointed to the ground and said, "Look, Mommy…Love." And there it was. A perfect little yellow heart-shaped leaf. A perfect reminder that no matter what, love is always there. I scooped him up in my arms and hugged him so tight, that I thought I would never let him go. And I haven't. He is almost twelve now and my biggest teacher. He is my greatest gift and my Guardian Angel.

Thankfully, Michael doesn't remember much of his first year of life because neither do I. It was the darkest, scariest and most painful year of my life. I just had my miracle baby, who I wanted more than anything on this earth. However, instead of feeling joy and love, I now had no idea who I was, besides anxious, lost, feeling alone and suicidal. I could not "snap out of it" or "get over it," like some friends told me to, in order to properly take care of my son. They didn't understand how I could feel so low, after experiencing the miracle of life and soon became disappointed in me. I wanted to scream, run far away and give up completely. I felt stuck in my mind and body. No amount of yoga, deep breathing or meditation could fix me. I knew something was horrifically wrong. Fear deeply set in. I wanted a way out. Thoughts led to killing myself, before Michael could get to know me. My family could raise him. He would be fine. And I could stop all these obsessive thoughts, mental and physical pain and sleepless nights of many tears. However, then I miraculously made it to my six-week OBGYN appointment, who immediately referred me to a psychiatrist. I was quickly diagnosed with Postpartum

Depression and Anxiety, as well as Post Traumatic Stress Disorder and began talk therapy and medication.

You see, my pregnancy and Michael's birth almost cost me my life. I had a high-risk pregnancy with him after two previous miscarriages as well as the surgical removal of my ovary, fallopian tube and a grapefruit-size ovarian cyst. My chances of actually carrying him to term were slim. During the pregnancy, I also had pre-eclampsia and cholestasis of the liver, and almost stroked out during the c-section. Now I was feeling all the effects, mentally and physically.

Postpartum Depression affects millions of women each year around the world and sometimes, unfortunately, without proper diagnosis and treatment. Sadly, too many succumb to suicide. Luckily, my doctor and family recognized the signs and got me the help I needed. It was a long road and a tough year, but I survived and recovered. I am forever grateful to my healing tribe.

As I learned about and recovered from my mental illness that year, three things saved my life:

Therapy and Medication

I put this on the top of my list. This is because without my obstetrician, psychiatrist and medication, I wouldn't be alive today. In my case, medication and therapy were necessary for recovery. I learned to release my shame of needing to see a therapist and asking for help, when I felt I was supposed to be strong for me and my baby. My psychiatrist helped bring me back to me, at a time when I completely forgot who I was. I also want to give many thanks to the post-partum depression support group at Tri-City Family Services in Geneva, IL. Just to be with other mothers going through the same thing, helped me breathe and feel human again. I'm still in therapy today but off all medication. Because of my experience, I am a huge advocate of the importance of medication and talk therapy for mental illness, as well as vulnerability and telling your story to others. You never know when sharing the experience of the worst time of your life can be a lifesaver for someone else.

Family and Friends

I am extremely lucky to have the best and most supportive family and friends in the world. My mother and my sister are saints, because they always go out of their way to be there for me and Michael. They truly love us unconditionally. In those first few weeks after I gave birth, my mom rarely left my side. She just knew I needed someone. It meant the world to me. Her love saved me. We now live with my mom and I wouldn't change a thing. She is my best friend and Michael adores her. I couldn't do what I do now without her. More on that in a bit…

I also wouldn't have survived that first year without my dear friend, Katie, who picked up the phone at 3a, listened without telling me what to do or how to feel and never judged me, only loved. I am alive because of her support, compassion and big hugs. And she's a mom too, so she gets it.

In the end, I can't emphasize enough the importance of a trusted and loving support system. You need to have people who can be honest with you, cry with you, listen to you and just sit with you in your darkness without judgment. Don't be afraid to honestly open up. Tell them how you feel. Tell your doctor how you feel. Don't hide or run. Your tribe will find you anyway, if you do. Thank goodness for that.

Yoga and Meditation

My professional background is in television/film production and marketing/fundraising, so my life consisted of long hours and stressful deadlines for many years. I was first diagnosed with panic disorder almost 20 years ago, so it was no surprise when I started to have anxiety after giving birth. I just didn't know that it would escalate to a level I couldn't handle myself. When I was first diagnosed with panic disorder, my doctor prescribed meditation every day and yoga three times a week. In the beginning, I thought it was all so silly and pointless. First, I didn't have time to exercise and second, I don't sit still, like ever. I was so annoyed when I entered the yoga room and rolled out my mat at the Batavia Park District on a frigidly cold day two decades ago. I kept thinking of all the things I had to do. I didn't have time to focus on me and my body. My emotions escalated. Then the instructor said, "You have the right to feel the way you do." I had an ah-ha moment. The tears began to flow. I looked up. Stained glass windows. Was this an old church? I prayed. Then my life completely changed.

I continued to work in television for 10 years after my first yoga class, but I was better equipped to handle the stress. I worked with the most talented producers, won two Midwest Emmys and taught television studio production to high school students, something I thought I would never do. I was blessed to have successfully worked so many years on television. Through it all, I continued to practice yoga. Yoga taught me to love myself through all emotions and love my body through all its changes. Because of my high-risk pregnancy, it was too risky to practice yoga or exercise at all. I then learned mantra (chanting), pranayama (breathwork) and meditation. I was hooked. However, once I gave birth, I had no passion for anything yoga. This was also a huge sign to me that something was wrong, and I needed help. After the therapy, medication and support, I was able to attend yoga again. I was motivated and excited. The owner at Heaven Meets Earth Yoga in Evanston, IL noticed my passion and asked if I ever thought about becoming a yoga teacher. Yes, many times. Teacher training started the next Monday. That Monday was my birthday. I took it as a sign, quit my television job and the rest is history.

I graduated yoga teacher training right after Michael turned one. I began teaching yoga full-time and loved my newfound purpose. My mom watched Michael while I taught, or some studios allowed him to be with me in class. I felt so blessed and was sure that I had found my path. I was happy and fulfilled. About three years into teaching Hatha, Vinyasa, Prenatal, and Restorative Yoga, I decided to sign up for Kundalini Yoga Teacher Training at Spirit Rising Yoga in Chicago, IL. It was the hardest and most rewarding thing I have ever done in my life. My teachers taught me to live my truth and heal into the best person I can be. Kundalini is my home and the community members are my family. Michael has really been raised by my entire family and yoga tribe, to whom I attribute his kindness, compassion, and a huge heart. I absolutely love teaching yoga. It's what I was born to do. I still teach yoga full-time in the Chicagoland area, focusing on mental health and wellness. I also host numerous yoga retreats in Illinois and soon to be Maine. If it wasn't for my mental illness and diagnosis, I don't think I would have ever practiced and ended up where I am today.

Back to that little yellow heart leaf. I now notice hearts wherever I go. In nature, artwork, sidewalks, clouds. Everywhere. Love is all around us and within us. We are love. We are loved. We are loving. No matter how we are feeling. No matter the circumstances. No matter what. We are loved and supported. We are never alone. It took the worst year of my life to teach me that most important lesson.

Namaste and Sat Nam

Jenny Bergold

Jenny Bergold (Jagatjeet Kaur) started practicing yoga in 1999. She began teaching yoga in 2009. Jenny discovered that it calmed the body and strengthened the mind. Jenny has her 200-Hour Hatha certification from Heaven Meets Earth Yoga in Evanston, IL and her 200-Hour Kundalini certification from Spirit Rising Yoga in Chicago, IL. She is also certified in Prenatal, Restorative, Yin, and Radiant Child Yoga. Jenny's classes focus on the mind and meditation, healing the body through asana, and uplifting the spirit through inspiration. Before teaching yoga, Jenny produced television programs for WTTW/Channel 11 in Chicago, IL and BATV/Batavia Access Television in Batavia, IL. She also has an extensive marketing and fundraising background. Her awards include two Midwest Emmys for Associate Producing ArtSafari and Trinity Irish Dance Company: One Step Beyond. Jenny lives in Elburn, IL with her mom, Kathy and son, Michael.

Jenny Bergold

Light of the World Yoga

42W566 Pouley Road

Elburn, IL 60119

630-465-1243

JennyJagatjeet@hotmail.com

Morgan Heuschmidt-Zorn

God's Warrior

It was Sunday, October 23rd, 2016. I was on Cloud 9. Nothing could stop me. I was in the car with my fiancé Eric, leaving my college graduation party. The sun was beautiful; shining through the car windows on my face. I closed my eyes. Here I was. After six long and hard years; I was officially done with college and had obtained my BFA in Interior Design. My dream had come true. It was hard to believe at first, that I actually made it. You see, I have been sick for many years. I have quite a few "invisible illnesses," as they are called because you can't see that I am sick. I currently suffer from anxiety, asthma, Chronic Fatigue Syndrome, Cushing's Disease, depression, fibromyalgia, OCD, Polycystic Ovary Syndrome, PTSD, restless leg syndrome and thyroid disease.

We were on our way to Top Golf for an after-party that one of our best friends, Bob, who worked there, was throwing for me. Surrounded by friends, we had an incredible night. When it was almost time to leave, I looked around and thought—"wow, how blessed am I?" I gave Bob a huge hug and kiss on the cheek, thanking him for everything he had done. We all said our goodbyes and went our separate ways. Little did I know, I would be falling off that cloud way sooner than I could have ever imagined.

On Thursday, November 3rd, I received a phone call from Eric, while he was at work, that I never expected. Bob had passed away in his sleep on Monday, October 31st, 2016. Bob had been in and out of the hospital quite a few times that summer, due to health complications. All these thoughts flooded my head- "This isn't real. It's a bad dream I'll be waking up from anytime soon. There has to be a mistake. I just saw him. We were just snap chatting on Saturday"! However, it was reality. In the blink of an eye, the world had suddenly become darker. This was because one of the friendliest, most loving, best people in the world was no longer in it. He was now an angel. We remember and honor him by sharing stories, favorite memories and photos.

We rolled into 2017, which was the year Eric and I were getting married, on Saturday, December 23rd, 2017. We still had quite a bit of time before our big day. I had not been feeling the best nor had my dad. He was diagnosed with mild Dementia / Alzheimer's in 2015. It was a struggle. My father, who was a very independent and talented man, was now taking medicine which he hated and also started having frequent in and out hospital stays. My mom, dad, Eric and I decided to make a change and move from Schaumburg to St. Charles, Illinois. We agreed on an in-law living arrangement. My mom saw changes coming with my dad and in the house that we chose, there was a guest bedroom with a bathroom that a caretaker could stay in, when it got to the point of my dad needing full-time care. I was in complete denial, however. In my mind, this was just a new chapter in our lives, in a new town, with us staying together. He was still doing most of the things he had always been doing. It was maybe a little different, but nonetheless, my dad was still fine in my eyes.

Fast forward to September of 2017. We had officially closed on our new home and moved in! The first morning there, all four of us stood by the front door and held hands, while my mom said a beautiful prayer. There were boxes everywhere and we had our work cut out for us. We needed the house unpacked and set-up by November, because we were having my bridal shower here. We managed to pull it off by the last minute and everything was beautiful. We were full of excitement, since our wedding was next month!

On Thanksgiving, my dad was not himself at all. He could hardly walk. Days went by and he was getting worse. For the past few months, I had put my health on the backburner to focus on my dad and the wedding. December came and we woke up one morning to find my dad extremely ill. He was taken to the hospital and was admitted. I was getting nervous. "Is my dad going to be able to walk me down the aisle"? "Is he even going to be healthy enough to be at the wedding"? I kept getting reassured by family, friends and even the doctors that he would be better by the 23rd and would be walking me down the aisle. I prayed and worked on wedding things to keep myself busy.

On Tuesday, December 12th at four in the morning, my mom got a phone call from the hospital. My dad had flatlined. It took 10 minutes to bring him back and we needed to get to the hospital ASAP. In total shock, I got dressed and we notified our family and close friends of what had happened. That week is a bit of a blur for me. We went back and forth to the hospital, talking to numerous doctors and so on. He had pneumonia and his body was not responding to the antibiotics. We were also told that since he was without oxygen for 10 minutes, his Dementia / Alzheimer's was no longer mild. It was more than likely to the point, where he would not know who any of us were. The decision was made to postpone our wedding. There was no possible way we would be able to celebrate our marriage, knowing the state my dad was in.

It was now Thursday, December 14th. Our family was in a private room, where we could talk. I remember going up to my brothers and saying, "dad is dying". It finally hit me. He would not be walking me down the aisle, attending my wedding, or any of the plans we had made when we moved to St. Charles. My mom, who was a Hospice CNA before, made the decision to put dad on Hospice. I had one wish before my dad left this Earth. I wanted him to know that his baby girl had married the love of her life. That Thursday night, we called our pastor who was going to marry us and we had a bedside ceremony. We were in dad's ICU room surrounded by some of our family and best friends. I stood by his bed, holding his hand as our vows were said. It was the most bittersweet moment ever. Even though my dad was not coherent; I knew that in his heart he witnessed us get married. On Friday, December 15th, 2017, my dad gained his wings and was free of all pain.

The first few months of 2018 were unbearable. I was extremely depressed and didn't want to leave the house. However, I knew that I still had to live my life. That is what daddy would have wanted. Spring came and I was trying to adjust to this "new normal". We had picked a new wedding date- Saturday, July 14th, 2018. Preparations had begun again for the wedding. However, this time I was asking for more help than before. In May, I had been in the hospital twice. I was beyond exhausted and constantly getting sick. Another path began to unfold. We made it to the wedding. It was the most magical day ever. We honored my dad and Bob in many ways, including special place settings. Eric and I had an incredible honeymoon in San Diego, California. On the flight home, I started to feel like I was getting sick again. 72 hours later, I was in the ER. Enough was enough. Specialist doctors were found, appointments were made and tons of tests were done. I was like a human pin cushion, having my blood drawn so often. The endocrinologist then gave us the news that he had suspected. I had a tumor on my pituitary gland in my brain. It resulted from having Cushing's Disease. I needed to have surgery to remove it. I had never had surgery before. My first one was going to be brain surgery.

My surgery was scheduled for Friday, January 25th, 2019. My mom, Eric, my sister, her boyfriend and I spent the holidays at Walt Disney World. When the vacation was over, it was more tests to prep and prepare for surgery. January 25th finally came. Eric, my mom and I left the house at five in the morning to head to the hospital. I was put in a pre-op room to get everything ready. I was so scared that I started to cry and pray. "Please God and Jesus, daddy, Bob, all my angels, let the surgery be successful". I kissed Eric and my mom and was wheeled into the operating room. "I'm going to start giving you the anesthesia now, Morgan". "Imagine you're on your way to San Diego; relaxed, going to the beach…" said one of the doctors. His words faded and I was out. A few hours later, I heard my name being called, as I was waking up from the surgery. Once the anesthesia wore off, I was told the surgery was a success. They were able to remove the tumor. I had one more hurdle to get through, however. The tumor was being sent to a lab to get tested to see if it was cancerous. Hallelujah! It was not! I spent five days in the ICU. When I was finally released to go home, I was very relieved. I couldn't wait to see my fur/feather babies again. I was on strict bed rest for eight weeks. I thought to myself, "the hardest part is done, it's smooth sailing from here on out". Oh, was I wrong! I had lost my sense of smell and taste and my other senses were slightly affected too. I had horrible insomnia sometimes, while other times I was sleeping the entire day. I was extremely weak. There were multiple follow-up appointments, I had pain and my emotions were all over the place. The doctors explained that since I had this tumor on my brain for so long, my body and brain were mad that it was no longer there. Therefore, I was dealing with a handful of "side effects," you could call them. Family and friends often came over to visit, which always lifted my spirits.

Month after month, slowly but surely, I am getting better. I still see doctors frequently and am in physical therapy to help get my strength back. Yes, I will still have these invisible illnesses. Some days are great. I feel well and am able to do things. Some days are not so great and I cannot even get out of bed. However, on both the good and bad days, I am very thankful that I am still here. God has blessed me with the best support group of family and friends. My number ones are my husband and my mom. I always keep my faith and try to stay as strong as possible. I refuse to let my illnesses stop me from living. They might slow me down sometimes, but they will never take me down. I am a fighter. *"God gives his toughest battles to his strongest soldiers"*. Throughout this journey, I have grown, changed and learned a lot. Life is hard and full of ups and downs that we cannot see coming, nor can we control. Believe in your dreams and go after them, love with all your being, and NEVER give up without a fight.

Thank You

To my amazing, loving and supportive husband; you are my soulmate always and forever.

To my mommy; you truly are an Angel on earth, for all that you've done and do for people, especially me.

I love you both so much.

Dedication

To my father; Donald Anthony Heuschmidt.
I will always be daddy's girl.

To Robert Ridgeway; you are one in a million.

We love and miss you both and know you are always with us.

Morgan Heuschmidt-Zorn

Born and raised in Schaumburg, Illinois, Morgan grew up living with her mom, dad and older sister, Brittnee. She also has two half-brothers; Michael and Timmy. She attended college at The Illinois Institute of Art-Schaumburg. She was a Dean's Honor List student and in 2017 received the Steven Kolton Award for outstanding leadership. She graduated with her bachelor's degree in fine arts, with a concentration in Interior Design. Morgan is an independent Interior Designer, currently working on building her own business. When Morgan's mom was a Hospice CNA, Morgan volunteered at the memorial services for Provena Hospice in Frankfort, Illinois.

In Morgan's free time, she'll often be using her creativeness; working on interior design projects, crafting, writing, painting or sewing. She is a fur/feather mama to 7 babies; 3 dogs, 2 parakeets, 1 Quaker parrot and 1 sugar glider. Morgan loves animals and her babies are her life! Weekends are filled with spending time with family and friends. Morgan prefers reading over watching television but makes an exception when it comes to watching her and her husband Eric's favorite TV show; Bob's Burgers. She is a Disney fanatic! She also loves the water and considers the ocean her "peaceful place". Faith is very important to Morgan; guiding her through the good and bad times. She is always counting her blessings!

Morgan Heuschmidt-Zorn
Morgan HZ Designs
4N071 Trotter Lane
Saint Charles, IL 60175
847-450-8670
m_heu@outlook.com
Morganhz.com

Michelle Jenks

We All Have a Story

It wasn't unusual for me to get asked to stay after school, especially in middle school. It didn't happen every day, but often enough that we had a house rule made just for me. It said that if you got detention, you walked the two miles home. You did not call for a ride.

It was one of those days in the middle of winter. I sat in detention with a dozen or so kids. This day was different. I was released before anyone else. The teacher thought he was doing me a favor. He wasn't. He was forcing me to walk alone. I tried to take my time gathering up my books and pens, as the other kids jeered. Some complained that things weren't fair. I agreed. However, eventually I had to leave. I took my time walking the halls, hoping for someone to join me on the walk home.

The halls were unusually empty that day. Teachers usually left together, band students carried or half-dragged their instruments toward the doors and janitors pulled their mops and large trash cans from room to room. However, on that day, the halls were empty.

My steps echoed, as I walked. It made me uncomfortable. I had no tangible reason to feel nervous. These were halls that I walked every day. But that day I felt alone and incredibly vulnerable. I hated that feeling. I hated it even more when he suddenly appeared. He was in front of me before I realized anyone was in the hall with me. That terrified me. I jumped. I could tell that pleased him. I knew a game that I did not want to play, was about to start.

"Whatcha doin' here all by yourself?" he taunted. "You know these halls aren't safe after school."

I talked back. That's what I had learned to do: act tough and they usually backed off. It didn't work this time. He kept taunting. He had me. We were the only two in the hall. It was silent, except for his mocking words. I don't know how he managed to move me closer to the wall and boys' bathroom, as he gained leverage. However, in no time at all, I felt cornered. He grabbed the stack of books in my arms and threw them into the boy's bathroom.

"You want them back, pretty girl?" he asked. "You know what you can do for them."

This game went on for a while. I asked for my books back, while he danced like a boxer in front of the bathroom door and told me all the things I could do to get them back. He used the most vulgar language to convey the "deal" he was offering. When I'd refuse, he'd just dance a step closer and say he could just take it if he wanted. When he got close enough, his dance included rough touches that I tried to swat or turn away from.

The longer it went on, the more vulnerable and scared I felt. My anger grew. I felt rage at seeing no students, no janitors, no teachers. I was angry at my fear that was keeping me from thinking clearly. I was angry that he thought he could get away with this. Rational and irrational thoughts flooded my mind. The loudest one was to fight back. That is what I did.

Then it all changed as quickly as it had started. Elijah came walking down the hall. He was my friend. Elijah had been bussed to my grade school, in an effort to desegregate the town. We played during recess. We'd often get sent to the principal's office for roughhousing. I'd get released to my classroom, while he'd wait patiently to see the principal, until one day I waited and marched into the principal's office with him and said, "If he gets in trouble, so do I. He didn't hurt me. We were playing together. He's my friend." It was the last time either of us got sent to the office.

Elijah was soon standing about five feet away from us. He looked at me, looked at him and back at me. In one fell swoop, he pinned the guy to the wall with one hand and reached out to touch my arm with his other hand, as I straightened my clothes.

"You okay?" he asked. I nodded. Elijah told me to get my books. I walked into the bathroom and wanted to cry, seeing them spread all over the floor. The book covers I had spent hours making were ripped and torn. Pencils and pens were scattered across the floor. They looked defiled, sitting cockeyed in the questionable puddles on the floor. I left them there to be swept away.

After I returned and stood across the hallway, Elijah turned back to the boy in his grip and said, "You don't mess with her ever again, you hear? You ever touch her, I'm coming for you." He dropped his hand, walked over to me, put his arm around my shoulder and walked me away.

Elijah walked me all the way home. He walked me in the cold over two miles in the opposite direction of his house. We didn't talk once about what had happened. I didn't speak about it with anyone. I didn't tell my sisters, my parents, not even a single friend. I walked inside my house, made myself a snack and went to my room to do my homework. It was hours, before I felt my body stop shaking.

Unfortunately, my experience isn't abnormal. Middle school is hard. I've sat with countless women, listening to their stories, with tears rolling down their faces, as they told me of having to change schools in junior high, because of mistreatment. They talked about their feelings of being unknown, about their thoughts of suicide, or how they still carry shame because of the choices they made to be sexually active at a young age or their stories like mine with far worse outcomes.

We all have a story. Many of them are rooted in junior high, because of the many changes around that time. Brains go from thinking in mostly concrete ways to beginning to think abstractly, hormones rage through bodies like tsunamis and self-esteem barely holds on. Self-esteem, which has been at its highest right before puberty, plummets to its lowest when puberty hits. This low self-esteem takes root between the ages of 8-14 and it will stay at that level, until a girl or boy is in their 30s. It can sometimes last until their 40s, if they do not purposefully work on developing it. In other words, at the tender ages between 8–14, a child's self-esteem takes root and it will be 15–30 years before it has a real shot of changing on its own.

I believe that we have confused a couple of truths which perpetuate this low self-esteem. The good news is, it doesn't take a miracle to put things back to where they are supposed to be, whether we are still in our early teens, in the middle of our life or near the end.

I believe that self-esteem is a combination of self-worth and self-confidence. However, we often equate them, instead of seeing them as two complementary weights on a scale. Self-worth is the sense of value we give to ourselves at our core. It involves both thoughts and emotions. It influences how we perceive others and interact with the world. That sense of self or core is not dependent or connected to anyone or anything. It's not being a daughter or son, mom or father, entrepreneur or factory worker, spouse or sibling or an employer or employee. Some of us recognize our value, while others have a hard time.

This often gets confused with self-confidence, which is a measure of faith in our abilities. In other words, the sense of our ability to do something or succeed at something, gives us a sense of self-confidence. This is directly tied to some behavior such as: I can play the guitar, I can play soccer, I can empathize, or I can lead.

Here's the rub: focusing solely on self-worth actually lowers self-esteem. In the same way, focusing solely on self-confidence lowers self-esteem. Sadly, we tend to oversimplify and focus on just one. We may have been taught that we are valuable, just because we are who we are. Our parents or someone significant in our lives told us we were unique and lovable and important. We may have learned at a young age that we were good at math, or good at a sport, or funny, or had some skill that we got a lot of attention doing. We, therefore, learned that we were special because of that ability we had, and our self-confidence soared. However, if we didn't hear that we were valuable just because we were us and also recognized for our abilities in something, if we weren't taught to have a sense of self-worth and self-confidence, our self-esteem took a hit. We need a balance and ability to focus on both self-worth and self-confidence at the same time.

When I was cornered in the hall by the boy in junior high, I assumed I deserved it. I assumed I had done something to provoke him. My self-worth was low enough that I took the blame for someone else's poor choices. My self-confidence could have been sky high, but it didn't raise my self-esteem. I lived with the guilt of what happened for seven years. I told no one about what happened, until I had to write an autobiographical story in college. The telling of the story began a decade of discovering what I believed my worth was. It took a lot of work on my part to change my thinking and change the level of self-esteem I had carried since I was 12.

I believe one of the reasons that self-esteem will not change without intentional work, has to do with something called the Reticular Activating System (RAS). It's a bundle of nerves at our brain stem that filters out unnecessary information, so that we notice what is important to us. This occurs when we get a new car and then all of a sudden start noticing how many similar cars there are on the streets, or when we're in a crowd with lots of noise but can hear someone call our name.

In the same way, the RAS seeks information that validates our beliefs. If we have a belief that we don't deserve attention or don't count, our RAS will find information that confirms that belief. If we believe we are good at a certain behavior, our RAS will find information to confirm that. It's the way it was intended to function.

Therefore, if we want to change our self-esteem, or change the self-esteem of the children in our lives, all we have to do is build new neuropathways. We can do that by changing how we talk to and about ourselves. We can watch who we surround ourselves with. We can change what we focus on. Here are five things that I have found to be useful to change my neuropathways:

1. Write in a journal daily. Include three things you are grateful for and one affirmation that you repeat daily for 30 days.

2. Practice accepting compliments, instead of brushing them off.

3. Identify a behavior or activity you want to learn and take the time to develop it.

4. Find someone(s) who takes delight in you and spend time with that person often.

5. Volunteer and give back regularly.

Whether we are walking through middle school hallways, corporate corridors or city streets, we have the choice to control our internal dialogue and develop our self-esteem or let others tear it down. We decide what we are worth. We decide to claim our abilities. That choice affects how we relate to others. I am a firm believer that we need more Elijahs in the world and in our heads.

Michelle Jenks

    Michelle Jenks is the founder and Executive Director of The FUSIoN Project, a non-profit (501c3) organization that builds self-esteem in junior high school girls, with the intent to empower them and diminish the potential of victimization. She openly shares that she didn't set out to start a program for junior high girls. Her desire was to help women who had been sex trafficked. As she heard more and more about this horrific epidemic, she felt compelled to join the fight. After years of searching for her place in that world, she was awakened one night with the idea that she could do something to prevent more girls from needing recovery. Since the average age of someone who is sex trafficked is 12–14, she chose to work with that age group—junior high. She can no longer imagine her life without these amazing girls. Michelle has long been concerned about the victimization of women and girls. She is driven to make an impact in as many lives as she can in her lifetime. She combines skills she has acquired through her varied background that includes being a high school youth group director, co-creator and developer of a bi-annual teen convention, volunteer coordinator for two rape crisis centers, corporate trainer and speaker, entrepreneur and church consultant. When Michelle is not speaking to groups, leading The FUSIoN Project programs or consulting, she chooses to spend her time with her family. She has been married to her husband Roger for 24 years. They love to go on adventures and hike around the United States. They have a total of five children and nine grandchildren, whom they cannot imagine life without.

Michelle Jenks
The FUSIoN Project
P.O. Box 528
Oswego, IL 60543
630-402-6050
Michelle@FUSIoN4Girls.org
www.FUSIoN4Girls.org

Deborah Wilkinson Brown

Check Yourself

It is very important to have good credit. It defines who you are. As a Certified Credit Counselor, I speak to many people who are in debt and cannot obtain credit due to their credit scores. Some feel as though there's nowhere to turn. Life throws many curve balls and emergency situations arise. Once married, now divorced, it was difficult adjusting from a two-person household income to a one-person household income. Even though the income was less, the bills were the same and they came due every thirty days. With only one income, my bills became delinquent and it was very difficult to catch up. Accounts were obviously sold to collections agencies, then reported to the credit bureaus. My credit scores plummeted. I thought that by obtaining a loan to resolve the issues, the problems would be fixed. However, I didn't realize that I was getting deeper into debt. I later found myself obtaining another loan to pay off the previous loan. It was a vicious cycle.

After changing careers in order to increase household income, I eventually got my bills on track and felt as though everything was going great. I was able to pay bills as they arrived in the mail and had extra money for entertainment. I was working as a qualified professional and making decent money at the time. One day I arrived at work and was told by my manager to turn in my cellphone and my keys immediately. The company had to be out of the building by midnight. My job ended in a matter of seconds. There was no warning at all. My world was crushed. How would I pay my bills including: mortgage, car payment, utilities, food, gas and so forth? There were very little savings and I knew that the emergency fund would run out quickly. I had one son in college and one son at home. My first thought was, what am I going to do?

As a firm believer in Christ, I quoted to myself the scripture, Philippians 4:13, "I can do all things through Christ which strengthens me". The next few months were difficult, and a full-time job was very hard to find. I accepted a part-time job with a much lower salary than I was earning before. I managed to pay my mortgage and car payment in a timely manner. However, my credit cards became delinquent and were eventually sold to collection agencies again. My credit was impacted negatively. I knew that rebuilding my credit scores would be a struggle.

I didn't realize the extent of the damage I had incurred and the effects that it had on my credit report. I was being denied for everything I applied for. It was then when I knew that changes had to be made. I needed to quickly come up with a plan. I didn't like the feeling of being deprived. My goal was to create a monthly budget as a tool to help track household expenditures and unnecessary spending. The monthly budget would be my tool toward building good credit. The budget would provide a blueprint of how to decrease overspending, to possibly free up money that could be put towards paying off debts. I focused closely on sticking to my budget.

While on my journey towards improving my financial situation, I searched for ways to improve my credit score and to build a good credit history. This included opening a new credit card account with a small limit, becoming an authorized user and requesting a credit limit increase on my current cards. I became very proficient in my quest towards overcoming my obstacles.

One key to establishing good credit is to understand the credit report. The credit report is a statement about credit activity and credit situations. The credit report consists of several components. It includes the credit score, account histories, public records, personal information and inquiries. Each component plays a very important role. The credit report is used by creditors, lenders, banks, utility companies, organizations and employers to make mindful decisions of one's creditworthiness and trustworthiness. It is possible to obtain a free copy of the credit report each year, by visiting www.annualcreditreport.com. By checking my credit report, I would be able to identify any possible errors. Common errors on credit reports include; wrong names, phone numbers, addresses and accounts listed on the report with the same names (i.e. John Sr or John Jr). If errors are found on the credit report, you may dispute the error by writing a letter or calling the credit bureau in which the error appears. You may be required to provide some type of proof, in order to resolve the issue.

I needed to increase my credit scores. Credit scores are three-digit numbers that predict how likely you are to repay back a debt on time. Credit scores may differ from bureau to bureau, because not all creditors report to every credit bureau. Items on the credit report such as, payment history, amount of debt, type of credit, length and inquiries are factored together to create a credit score. Credit scores can range from 300–850. The higher the score, the lower the risk. The national average FICO score is 695. Having a credit score between 700 to 800 is considered excellent credit. Scores between 600–700 are considered good credit and scores below 600 are considered fair credit. The FICO (Fair Isaac) score is the most widely used. The FICO bases its scoring model on credit reports obtained from all three credit bureaus. Companies, such as Credit Karma and Credit Sesame, offer credit scores. However, they are not the official FICO score. Another scoring model is the Vantage Score 3.0, which was launched in 2006. The Vantage Score is not used as often as the FICO.

Credit scores are used by companies to grant credit and credit limits. One should focus on building a good credit history, in order to achieve a good credit score. Ways to build credit scores are: pay your bills on time, avoid closing open accounts, don't max out credit cards, limit hard inquiries and pay attention to the debt to income ratios. A high credit score will allow more opportunities to obtain the things that you want and will make life simpler.

When Credit Becomes Overwhelming

My credit scores began to increase over time. Eventually, I was suddenly eligible for all kinds of credit offers. Many offers for credit cards, store cards and personal loans filled my mailbox. Individuals with higher credit scores may receive offers more often than others. Many people fall victim to these offers. Before long, credit limits are out of control. Some people may become overwhelmed and feel as though there is nowhere to turn. It is your responsibility to know when enough is enough. Some of the loans and cash advances offers, carry interest rates of five hundred percent or more. It is understood that emergencies happen, and money is not always available. Therefore, last resorts are to obtain payday loans and cash advances. To avoid these types of offers, I created an emergency fund, into which I put cash, every pay period. I also utilized a money savings app called Acorn. I borrowed money only when necessary and only when it could be paid back. Other ways that I handled credit card debts, was to hide the credit cards away, lock the credit cards in a safe, freeze the credit cards, or just cut the credit cards up. I understood that opening new credit accounts would generate an additional monthly payment. I made sure that the money was within the budget to cover the expense. Opening new accounts created various due dates. I made sure that I was tracking due dates to avoid late payments. I made it a habit of paying the debt off each month, so that it didn't carry a balance.

Overwhelming debt can cause stress, sickness, sleepless nights, depression and many ailments. By utilizing the monthly budget, it helped alleviate some of the stress and allowed me an opportunity to structure the debt as a visual picture of what's coming in and going out. I also enrolled in a debt management program that helped reduce interest rates, lower monthly payments, stop late fees, over-the-limit fees and get out of debt quicker. There are many companies that offer debt consolidation programs. These programs are used in lieu of bankruptcy. Before I enrolled in the debt management program, I made sure that the company was reputable. I read company reviews, visited the company's website and checked the Better Business Bureau status.

I did my research.

There are pros and cons to every debt management program. Some cons are that it impacts the credit report negatively, if additional credit is applied for, it may be declined due to the fact that enrollment on a debt management program is in existence. Another concern is that creditors look at each account on a case-to-case basis. Therefore, not all creditors will agree to the terms of the consolidation. The pros are that all unsecured debts (credit cards, collections, medical bills, and some personal loans) are consolidated into one monthly payment, interest rates and monthly payments are lowered and the timeframe to get out of debt is quicker. The program is very successful and helps millions of people get back on their feet financially. The debt management program is one of the best solutions for getting out of debt.

Not all accounts qualify for a debt management program. Secured debts; such as mortgages, car loans and some personal loans, are not allowed on a debt management program. This is because collaterals were listed on the credit application in order to obtain credit. Those accounts are usually referred to a financial institution for the purpose of obtaining a debt consolidation loan.

If debt management is not an option, there is always the self- management option. This option provides the individual with the tools to handle their personal finances. However, there are no guaranteed creditor benefits. All attempts are handled by the individual, without the help of a debt consolidation company. The individual makes all calls to creditors to negotiate terms and conditions of the debt, so that a reasonable payment or arrangement can be made. Creditors are often not willing to work with the individual. They would much rather work with a reputable debt management company. I downloaded free credit score monitoring apps such as; Credit Karma and Credit Sesame. I requested a copy of the credit report, at least every six months. If errors were found, I disputed them, so that they would be removed from the credit report promptly.

Recovering from overwhelming debt is not impossible. However, it takes time, commitment, consistency and perseverance. It can be done with proper planning and with the correct tool. I created a plan to pay down the debt and stuck to the plan closely.

In summary, paying debts on time helps to build good credit. Good credit will allow you the opportunity to receive lower interest rates and obtain anything that you desire. Building a great payment history will result in great credit scores. The higher the score, the lower the risk. Try to aim for scores that are considered good. Practice ways to keep the credit score in good standing. Remember, if you are feeling overwhelmed, there is hope. Consider using debt consolidation. Don't allow your credit to determine who you. First, you must check yourself.

Overcoming my obstacles made me more determined to heighten my vision of becoming an entrepreneur. My vision is to establish a financial service agency that will offer credit counseling, insurance options, financial educational courses and notary services. My desire is to help individuals become debt-free, live healthier financial lives and widen their knowledge about finances.

Deborah is a certified credit counselor (National Foundation of Credit Counselor). She also holds insurance licenses (life, health, property, casualty), and a Notary Public certification. She received an MBA degree from Strayer University and has completed doctoral courses in Business (Entrepreneurship) from Walden University. Deborah has worked in many capacities within the financial industry for over twelve years.

Deborah Wilkinson Brown

Deborah is a native of Charleston, South Carolina. She is the sixth of seven children. As a child, Deborah enjoyed reading, writing and dressing up. She was truly a "girly" girl. Her passion for cosmetics and fashion gave her the desire to become a model. However, there was one dilemma. Deborah was larger than the average model. Deborah was determined and did not let her size stop her. She enrolled in the John Roberts Powers School of Modeling and Acting and became a successful plus-size model in Raleigh and the surrounding areas. She attended the International Model and Talent Association convention in New York and won honorable mention awards in fashion print and runway. She appeared in the "Sister to Sister" magazine and participated in numerous fashion shows throughout North Carolina. She has been a judge for several beauty pageants. One of them was the Mrs. North Carolina beauty competition. Her most fame acclaim was being portrayed as an extra in the movie, "The

Portrait," featuring Lauren Bacall and Gregory Peck.

Deborah is a believer in Christ and is very active in her church. Her motto is, "I can do all things through Christ who strengthens me" Phillipians 4:13. She presently serves as the Chairman of the Greeter's Ministry, Youth Advisor, Small Group Leader and previously was a Church Announcer. She was the former Basileus to the Chi Iota chapter of Zeta Phi Beta Sorority Inc., in which she helped charter its first chapter on the campus of Baptist College (now Charleston Southern University).

Deborah later found an interest in the finance industry. First, she was a mortgage broker, and later an insurance agent. Deborah has been in the financial arena in many capacities for more than twelve years. She enjoys working with numbers and thinks that it's important to be financially literate.

Deborah holds a Bachelor of Science degree in Sociology from Charleston Southern University, an MBA degree from Strayer University and has completed doctoral courses in both Psychology and Business at Walden University. Deborah is presently a certified credit counselor (NFCC) at a local non-profit. She spends her days counseling individuals on debt consolidation, budgeting, and money management.

Deborah resides in Raleigh, North Carolina. She has two sons, John and Tristian, a grandson, Jamir, and a daughter-in-law, Natosha.

Deborah Wilkinson Brown
3749 Tryon Ridge Drive
Raleigh, NC 27610
919-706-2827
dwb7474@aol.com
www.DeborahWilkinsonBrown.me

Christie Rocco Moore

Breaking up with Limiting Beliefs

Three years ago, I took a leap of faith. I left my six-figure corporate career of more than 20 years to pursue my entrepreneurial dreams. I had spent most of those years climbing the corporate ladder, chasing titles and promotions. It was no longer fun, nor fulfilling.

I knew it was time to move on, so I jumped!

Everyone warned me that the transition from employee to entrepreneur would be impossible. However, I had a history of massive success, so I just thought they were haters.

The first business I had was extremely successful right out of the gate. So there. haters!

I had partnered with a long-time client, who had already built a successful agency. Therefore, it was relatively easy setting up my new division and offering my products to his established customer base. The program I developed grossed nearly $3 million in sales the first year, which to be honest, blew me away.

I was in complete awe over the instant success that had taken place. I was very grateful to have accomplished what everyone said would be impossible.

For the first time in a long time, I felt on top of the world. I was no longer a slave to corporate! I had done it. I was an entrepreneur!

Finally, I felt alive, happy and excited! I began living life on my terms and it was incredible. I never knew it was possible to live without stress and not be in a constant state of panic or unhappiness. Now that I had a taste of this life, I knew I could never return to corporate.

I couldn't believe, and certainly wasn't prepared for, what happened next.

Overnight, our largest client got sold and my part of the business was forced to close.

I was devastated.

It came as a complete shock, that in the blink of an eye, the fairy tale dream-come-true had ended. It was back to the drawing board.

I was broken and defeated. Every day I got up feeling like a complete failure. I had no business, no purpose and no idea what to do.

I had nothing left to give and found myself incapable of bouncing back, like I had always been able to do before.

A year and a half later, it hadn't gotten better. In fact, it had gotten progressively worse.

I exhausted my savings and cashed out my 401k. I accumulated forty thousand dollars in debt and owed ten thousand dollars in back taxes.

I had hit rock bottom.

This was unchartered territory for me. I had never experienced such a low point.

During this period, I had stopped and started numerous other businesses, only to be left feeling empty and uninterested. I found myself chasing every shiny new object possible, hoping to siphon some form of passion out of myself.

At one point, my parents looked at me and asked, "Are you done playing around now? You need to get a job and go back to work."

But no, I wasn't done.

I knew I wasn't ready to go "get a job." However, I felt ashamed and embarrassed by the situation I put myself in and didn't know what to do about it. All I knew was I couldn't give up.

For me, displaying vulnerability equated to weakness. What I didn't understand yet, was that it was actually my lack of self-confidence and insecurities talking.

I didn't want to admit that I needed help but it was my ego talking.

The problem was I had been thrown so far off my course, that I didn't know how to take back my power and be in control.

I witnessed other entrepreneurs being successful. Therefore, I began watching them, searching for the answers on how to get my ball rolling again.

Horrifyingly, one of the things I came to realize was that because I joined a successful agency instead of starting from scratch, I never actually experienced the hardships of an entrepreneur. I had skipped several steps of starting a business, such as developing a business plan, creating marketing strategies or even dealing with startup costs.

Looking back at it now, the only entrepreneurial steps I took to get started were printing business cards and buying some accounting software.

I had jumped right over the scariest part of being an entrepreneur: finding my own clients. My established partner simply walked me in the front door and made the introduction.

It's no wonder that when it all went away, I became lost, stuck and unsure how to proceed, once I was completely on my own!

I began my hunt for the process that I needed to follow to be the successful entrepreneur I knew was in me. Imagine my surprise when it turned out that it had little to do with what was going on around me...... It had EVERYTHING to do with what was going on inside of me.

One day as I continued to corner every successful entrepreneur I could find hoping for the insight to the secret sauce, I connected with someone who asked me a question I wasn't prepared for: "What limiting belief do you feel could be holding you back, from getting what you want and living the life of your dreams?"

I was dumbfounded. I didn't even understand the question. I tried to hide my blank stare.

I had no idea what a limiting belief was.

Was it a condition? Is it contagious? Could I contract it from another person? Was it political or spiritual? Was I going to need medication?

I had no idea.

This is how my introduction to limiting beliefs went:

You know how sometimes you meet someone and feel like you've been best friends forever? It is like you've always known them.

That's how it felt between me and the person who ultimately asked me that crazy question. We were happily going along chatting about kids and pets and traveling. She then threw this at me: "What limiting belief do you feel could be holding you back?"

I was not ready for my reaction.

I immediately broke into a complete body sweat. I was transformed into a little girl, and got that uncomfortable, tingly feeling all over my body. I instantly returned to feeling overwhelmed, ashamed and embarrassed. These were feelings that I didn't know I had been carrying for years.

Within seconds, tears started rolling down my face. The scariest thoughts I couldn't believe I was even admitting, started coming out of my mouth.

"It's not in the cards for me."

"I'm not good enough."

"I'm not smart enough."

"I don't deserve to be happy."

"There's no way I can do this."

"I don't trust women, they hate me."

"I don't have a college degree."

"I'm going to lose everything I have."

She consoled me by saying, "there's nothing special about you, you are just as deserving as anyone else."

"You've just discovered your limiting beliefs."

I froze and let it sink in. I wanted to believe that she was right. I deserve happiness, success and wealth, just like everybody else.

The conversation continued, as she went on to ask me more questions. I was intrigued and I was all-in!

Here it was – the secret sauce I had been looking for.

In alignment with my earlier epiphany that entrepreneurial success doesn't happen overnight, and though let's be honest here, I had hoped this one conversation would solve all of my problems……. I woke up the next morning knowing that if I truly wanted to experience the level of success I knew I could, I was going to have to make a long-term commitment to overcoming my limiting beliefs.

It wasn't going to be easy.

For years, I had been programmed to think all those terrible things about myself that had come spewing out of my mouth during the conversation the day before.

The truth was that not only didn't the problem develop overnight, it also wasn't going to be fixed overnight either. This time I was in it for the long haul.

The good news was as hard as the conversation was to have. It sparked the achiever in me that experienced all those successes in corporate and even my first "entrepreneurial" venture. It was time to go big or go home.

I went to work.

I immersed myself in audiobooks about every aspect of self-improvement I could get my hands on.

To help me keep a motivated pumped up feeling, I discovered my "fight song" and listened to it any time I felt myself slipping.

I picked my top 10 limiting beliefs and I turned them into positive affirmations.

I visualized myself living, as if I'd already conquered those fears.

I wrote my affirmations on sticky notes and posted them on the wall in my office. Each morning, I would meditate and read them out loud. Several times.

I did the work, even when I didn't believe any of it. I kept doing the work, until little by little some of my affirmations started to ring true.

I am enough.

I am an action taker.

I deserve wealth and success.

I am beautiful.

I am confident and smart.

I continue to experience realizations each and every day. It's astonishing to witness your very own transformation.

Somewhere between shiny object number 134 and my unwavering commitment to breaking through these invisible forces that had been ruining and running my life, not only were my limiting beliefs slowly falling away, but I found clarity.

In much the same way that this person came out of nowhere and changed the course of direction for my life, I knew I had to do the same for others.

Everyone has the ability to break up with their limiting beliefs and cross the bridge to their very own breakthroughs: to begin operating at a higher frequency and take their power back.

My transformation has significantly impacted my mind, my life, my health, my business and my relationship with my husband and children.

Not only did I realize I wasn't special, in terms of thinking I was undeserving and other people were, but also, there's nothing special about me that says I can accomplish breakthroughs and transformations that other people can't.

While certainly proud of my successes back in my corporate days, and even though it didn't all go as planned in my humble "entrepreneurial" beginnings, nothing can compare to the feeling of creating a light-bulb moment for others, the way one was created for me that fateful day when someone asked me:

"What limiting belief do you feel could be holding you back?"

To learn more about how I help women begin their transformation by breaking up with limiting beliefs so they can be *fearless, functional and financially free* and to take advantage of the free resources available, please visit me at www.ChristieRoccoMoore.com. I encourage you to take time for yourself, sit down with a warm drink and a comfy blanket and start truly thinking not only about what limiting beliefs are holding you back, but what your life would look like, if you broke up with them!

Christie Rocco Moore

Christie Rocco Moore, a speaker, author, and Mindset Coach, creates "light bulb" moments of clarity for women, so they can live life on their terms.

"Go Big or Go Home!" Christie Rocco Moore lives by this philosophy. She challenged societal bias and pursued her corporate career right after high school, without a formal college education. She believes that success lives on the other side of fear, hard work, and perseverance.

Upon reaching a 20-year milestone in her career and being recognized as 1 of the Top 25 Women in the Auto Industry by *Agent Entrepreneur Magazine*, Christie took a leap of faith and left a six-figure corporate career to pursue her entrepreneurial dreams.

Christie experienced instant success out of the gate. The program she developed grossed nearly $3 million in sales the first year. Overnight, Christie's fairy tale dream-come-true had ended, when her largest client was sold and she was forced to close her business.

Through this turbulent time of devastation, shame, and feeling like a complete failure, she discovered her limiting beliefs and gained clarity.

Her extensive corporate background in leadership, in conjunction with her own personal transformation, has led her to help women change the course of direction in their lives. This will enable them to begin to discard their limiting beliefs, operate at a higher frequency and take their power back.

Christie's magnetic and energetic personality is infectious. She enjoys spending time with her family and drinking wine outdoors.

Christie Rocco Moore
Christie Rocco Moore
4607 Osprey Lane
Plainfield, IL 60586
708-243-7393